DEVELOP YOUR IDEA!

Get off to a flying start with guided exercises, templates & resources for exploring new business ventures.

Author
K.N. Kukoyi

DEVELOP YOUR IDEA!

Get off to a flying start with guided exercises, templates & resources for exploring new business ventures.

FREE RESOURCES

There are a number of downloadable resources that come free with this book (numbered 1, 2, 3 and 5.) Here's the list and links to where you can find them:

- **FREE GIFT:** There is a free bonus chapter available to readers of this book called: *A brief time out,* which includes productivity tips and more.
  http://www.mylanderpages.com/donthireasoftwaredeveloperuntilyoureadthisbook/free-chapter
- **Free resource 1:** *Chapter challenges workbook.* A summary of all the challenges that appear in this book. Note down the actions you wish to take and set yourself due-dates to complete them!
  http://www.mylanderpages.com/donthireasoftwaredeveloperuntilyoureadthisbook/Free-resource-1
- **Free resource 2:** *10 x Trello boards*, for you to copy and use, including project management boards, a road map board, customer service boards and task prioritisation boards. Look for the **purple board** called ***Develop Your Idea! Planning board***:
  http://www.mylanderpages.com/donthireasoftwaredeveloperuntilyoureadthisbook/free-resource-2-trello-boards
- **Free resource 3:** *My PMI Log*, great for reviewing information, organising your thoughts and making decisions.
  http://www.mylanderpages.com/donthireasoftwaredeveloperuntilyoureadthisbook/Free-resource-3-pmi-log
- **Free resource 5:** *Customer profile template.*
  http://www.mylanderpages.com/donthireasoftwaredeveloperuntilyoureadthisbook/5-customer-profile-avatar

DEDICATION

For Irene.

I'd like to extend a heartfelt thanks to everyone that supported me during the launch of this book. You are all superstars!

OTHER BOOKS BY K.N. KUKOYI

Develop Your Idea! Get off to a flying start with your startup. Guided exercises & resources for exploring & validating new business ventures.
Got a business idea in mind? Let's test it out! Plan for success with the Develop Your Idea! book, an Amazon 5* rated best seller purchased by entrepreneurs in 12 countries. Research your business idea using the guided exercises, templates and resources provided.

Amazon reviews for Develop Your Idea!
"If you're considering a startup, the author shares a common goal and is looking to encourage and help you through the pre-startup process. I have had experience starting two software as a service companies...and I found very solid and practical advice in this book regarding how to go about validating your product idea and your potential customers...it is an easy and concise read."

Available at your local Amazon store, or via this universal link for all countries: http://mybook.to/Develop-Your-Idea-exercises-validating-ebook

*   *   *

Don't Hire a Software Developer Until You Read this Book. The handbook for tech startups & entrepreneurs (from idea, to build, to product launch and everything in between)
A best-seller in multiple business categories and multiple countries including the UK, US, Canada, Brazil and Australia, this is *the* software survival guide for startups, small businesses and entrepreneurs that want to start, or grow their tech business the smart way.
Learn what you need to know and do to get your software product built and successfully delivered into the hands of your customers.

Amazon reviews for Don't Hire a Software Developer Until You Read this Book
"The only problem with this book is that it didn't come sooner. As an

entrepreneur who went through this process blind, I can tell you that this book is a must have for any business in this day and age. This book would have prevented me from several mistakes that cost $$$. I recommend that you read this book from cover to cover—an ounce of prevention is worth a pound of cure!"

Universal link for all countries: http://myBook.to/Dont-Hire-Software-Developer-Until-ebook

Don't Buy Software for Your Small Business Until You Read this Book. A guide to choosing the right software for your company & achieving a rapid return on your investment.
Are you a small or medium sized business with plans to upgrade or replace your business software? If so, this book is for you!
Changing IT systems can be costly, time-consuming and complicated. This book will guide you through the pitfalls and risks of choosing a suitable software product that will deliver the benefits you want, explains the advantages and disadvantages of the available options and demonstrates how to secure a good return on your investment.

Amazon reviews for Don't Buy Software for Your Small Business Until You Read this Book
Coming soon! This book launches in June 2017.

Universal link for all countries: http://myBook.to/small-business-software-buyers-guide

All books are available in 13 Amazon marketplaces: the UK, US, Canada, Australia, Netherlands, Brazil, France, Germany, Spain, Italy, Japan, India and Mexico.

CONTENTS

INTRODUCTION

"Everyone can tell you the risk. An entrepreneur can see the reward."
- Robert Kiyosaki

In this book, we will be looking at a range of ways that you can carry out business, market and consumer research to skew your odds away from "risk" and towards "reward"!

In 2014, CB Insights, a tech market intelligence platform, ran a "post-mortem" analysis on the failure of 101 startups based on feedback from the founders:https://www.cbinsights.com/blog/startup-failure-reasons-top/

Fig 1. Source: CB Insights - Top 20 Reasons Startups fail

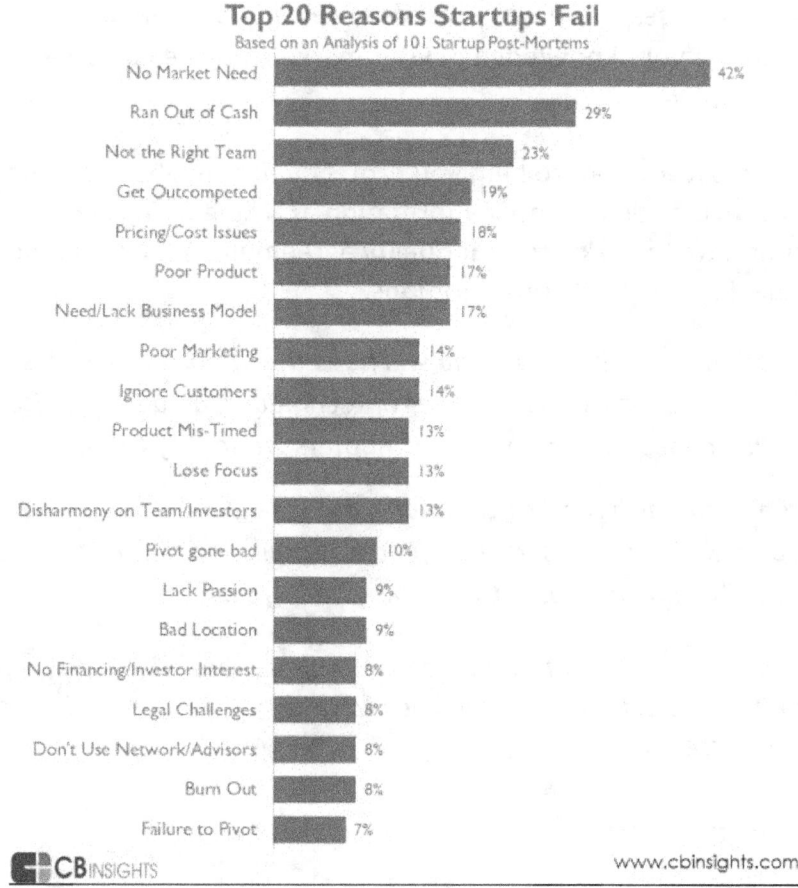

No market need is at number 1 on the list!

Do you find that as surprising as I do? Without a need for their product or service, the founders of new businesses are already fighting a losing battle.

Ignoring the customer is a reason provided by founders too, appearing at number 9 in the list!

Why, and how does this happen and what can we learn from this?

It's all too easy to get carried away with a business idea, however this idea needs to translate well into a tangible product that people can use and enjoy...and are willing to pay for! Even if people*are* interested, there need to be enough of those interested parties to sustain a business.

This book addresses these two reasons for business failure *and* will help you to increase your knowledge of your market and the customers that you wish to serve.

We will also cover topics to help you protect yourself when starting a new venture, including company formation, tracking of business expenditure, trademarks, confidentiality agreements and legal and Intellectual Property (IP) considerations.

As you read through this book, you will have the opportunity to research and refine your ideas using a number of techniques, guided exercises and Chapter Challenges, which appear in chapters 2 and 3 of this book.

*By the time you finish reading **Develop Your Idea!**, you should also have at least one mini business plan completed. Would you agree that these activities will bring you closer to reaching your goals?*

There is also a work book that you can download that will help you plan and prioritise the actions that you wish to take. (Continue reading to find out how to access it.)

I just love it when a plan comes together. I'm sure you do, too, so let's work on yours so you can make progress with researching, planning and developing your business idea!

* * *

I learned professional research skills and interview techniques as a market research executive. I would travel up and down the country running focus groups and interviewing everyone from consumers, to small business owners, to the Directors of multinational companies and even politicians at the Houses of Parliament. I have also run many sessions with business customers and members of the public for the purposes of gathering feedback about new software products.

I will be sharing my top tips with you!

I also have personal experience of creating a profitable "side-hustle" business, as well as larger scale ventures which I researched and analysed before starting. Call me a nerd, (maybe that's fair as I've spent over 10 years working in "techie roles") but I enjoy the research, planning and organisation side of starting a business and I'm not much of a fan of "winging it", or "leaping before looking." I always prefer a *safe bet* and I don't find the risk of losing money exciting!

As long as you don't get stuck in a loop where nothing else but daydreaming or mental preparation happens, your research should give you the ability to make good decisions and the confidence to get started. Research isn't everyone's cup of tea, but it *is* worth the effort, and the time you invest now will benefit you later! There is a very fitting quote from the author Sean Patrick Flanery that sums this up:

"Do something today that your future self will thank you for."

If you're interested in building software to sell, you may also wish to read *Don't Hire a Software Developer Until You Read this Book*: https://www.amazon.com/Dont-Hire-Software-Developer-Until-ebook/dp/B01LY5C1IK/, the handbook and software survival guide for technical entrepreneurs. In that book, we'll cover many subjects step-by-step, including: pricing models, marketing, product development, software quality, project management, product launches, customer care and the translation of ideas into requirements that you can discuss with a developer - one that I'll show you how to hire, and work with to build your app!

Please visit the Free Resources page to pick up the documents, tools and scripts that come free with this book to help you with your venture.

Good luck!

CHAPTER 1
Protecting your interests

In this chapter:

- Intellectual Property
- Non-disclosure agreements
- Trademarks
- Choosing a legal status for your company
- Insuring your business
- Accounting, budgeting and keeping financial records
- A brief word about VAT

Let's discuss these business fundamentals.

IMPORTANT: Laws and procedures may differ according to your country of residence. Please contact the equivalent bodies in your own country and when seeking professional advice, always use the services of lawyers and chartered or certified accountants authorised and qualified to practice in your country.

Intellectual Property

In order to protect your interests, you'll need to know about Intellectual Property (IP).

IP is an umbrella term which covers copyrights, patents, designs and trademarks and the laws and codes of practice related to them.

Fig 2. Types of IP. Source: The Intellectual Property Office (IPO)

Intellectual Property (IP) concerns creations of the mind. IP can be:

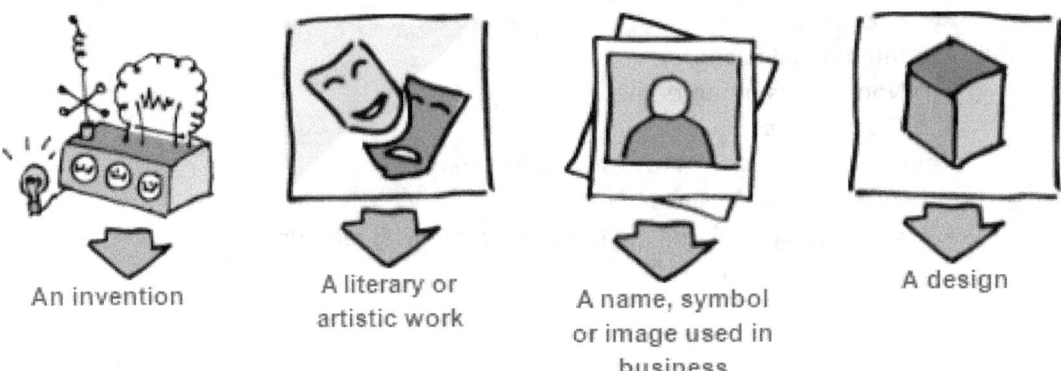

An invention

A literary or artistic work

A name, symbol or image used in business

A design

The Intellectual Property Office (IPO) is the government body responsible for intellectual property rights in the UK.

It's well worth contacting the IPO (or its equivalent in your own country) for some free advice. However, you may still need to seek advice from a solicitor. Familiarity with relevant trademark case law, recent disputes and an understanding of how these might be relevant to your individual case will be important, so if you hire a law firm, confirm that they are *specialists* in IP.

Patents, copyright and inventions

Regardless of where you're based, you can access free information about *patents, trade secrets*, and *trademarks* via the link below to see where your idea fits within the "big picture" of IP.

http://www.ipo.gov.uk/blogs/iptutor/stem-patents-and-trade-secrets-part-1/

This page from the IPO contains an IP overview, as well as links to specific IP topics:

https://www.gov.uk/government/organisations/intellectual-property-office

The IPO have produced a short video called "What's intellectual property got to do with me?"

You can access it here: https://youtu.be/PMab4oRGaZc.

It's just over 1 minute long and packs in a lot of information in a simple overview. With this information in mind, you should be more confident in approaching local channels regarding Intellectual Property related topics.

Legal documents and services

Non-disclosure agreements (NDAs)

Before you discuss your idea, make any verbal or written agreements, or hire anyone to join your business, **make sure you know where you stand in terms of Intellectual Property.** The IPO offers this advice:

Fig 3. Discussing your invention. Keeping Schtum! Source, The Intellectual Property Office (IPO)

If you have previously revealed your invention publicly in any way, you cannot patent it.

However, this does not mean that inventions cannot be discussed before a patent application is made.

There may be people you will need to discuss your invention, with such as:

- the development team
- an investor
- an IP professional (such as a Patent Attorney)

Before you discuss the details all parties should sign a 'Non-Disclosure Agreement' which can help to protect the secrecy of your invention.

You do not need a Patent Attorney to sign a **non-disclosure agreement** as they are subject to legal privilege.

NDAs (also described as secrecy or confidentiality agreements) are legal contracts which give you grounds to take action in court against those who break their terms. They may cover material, knowledge, processes or information about your idea or business activities and can be used if

17

you want to share your idea in order to get feedback, but wish to keep information about your company and its plans confidential.

The entrepreneurial community is divided about NDAs – some believe ideas are worthless and it is the *execution* of the idea that matters, whilst others believe that ideas can be valuable. You will need to decide where you stand on this matter and what you will do if people refuse to sign. Will you work with them, or choose to walk away?

There are a number of places online where you can access legal documents.

SEQ Legal offer a selection of free and pay-as-you-go legal documents for Internet and Business Law, including documents for those creating mobile apps, NDAs, software license agreements and more: http://www.seqlegal.com/

Elance, an online marketplace for freelancers has some sample NDA, project and freelancer agreements that you can review: http://help.elance.com/hc/en-us/articles/203735913-Sample-Contract-Agreements

Contractstandards.com, offers "standardised contracts, checklists, and clauses built with analysis of thousands of public documents" and has Website terms of Service, Privacy Policies, NDAs, Patent License Agreements and many other contractual documents that you can look at: https://www.contractstandards.com/contracts.

Docracy describes itself as "The web's only open collection of legal contracts and the best way to negotiate and sign documents online" and has contracts and agreements for hiring developers and designers, which you can find here: http://www.docracy.com/4754/contract-for-mobile-application-development-services

http://www.docracy.com/2817/standard-agreement-for-design-services-interactive-web-works-full-assignment

If you're UK based, *Lawbite* offers access to a range of legal documents on a pay-as-you-go basis for a one off cost of £99 + VAT including e-signing facilities and two free fifteen minute legal advice sessions: https://www.lawbite.co.uk and *Rocket Lawyer* charges £25 a month for access to legal documents and the ability to ask questions; https://www.rocketlawyer.co.uk/

The UK Government's gov.uk website has several versions of NDA available to view and download at: https://www.gov.uk/government/publications/non-disclosure-agreements.

 A few words of caution about contracts:

These links have been provided for your convenience.

If in doubt, please seek legal advice to ensure that your contract includes all the necessary clauses and caveats and is suitable for your specific situation.

You may also wish to seek advice to find out how an NDA might be enforced if you hire freelancers that are not based in the same country as you. In this case, you may need to confirm whether the laws of your home country are applicable to people living and working elsewhere.

Trademarks

A *trademark* is defined as a design, graphic, logo, symbol, word or phrase or any combination of these used to identify your business or product. If your trademark application is approved, this will allow you to use the registered trademark symbol, ®.

A list of trademark specialists can be found on *The Institute of Trade Mark Attorneys* website: http://www.itma.org.uk/members/

To see whether the company, product or brand name(s) you have in mind have already been trademarked, check the database of existing names and keywords here: https://www.ipo.gov.uk/tmtext.htm.

Companies House has a page to help you check whether the limited company name you want has already been taken - you cannot pick a name that has already been claimed. You can find it here: http://wck2.companieshouse.gov.uk//wcframe?name=accessCompanyInfo.

If you haven't got a name for your business or product yet, there's a thought-provoking process outlined here: http://www.nickkolenda.com/naming-process/.

The *Table of Contents* will show you the process broken down into sections, however this is not easy to find, so do a Control+F (or Command+F for Mac users) on the page to find it quickly.

Choosing a legal status for your company

There are a number of "business structures" or "legal statuses" you can choose, including *limited company, sole trader, partnership and social enterprise:*

A *limited company structure* "limits" your personal liability because the company is a legal entity - your finances and the company's finances are separate. This protects personal assets such as your home, car or other personal property in the face of legal action or bankruptcy, (although it's still essential to have the right insurance cover in place.)

A *sole trader's* assets *aren't* protected in this way - the individual and the business are not separate legal entities.

The Director(s) of limited companies are obliged by law to submit or "file" *annual returns* and *annual accounts* (replaced by *confirmation statements* as of June 2016) to Companies House; the UK body that forms and dissolves limited companies and registers and manages their data. As a limited company, you face fines and other penalties if you or your accountant do not file the required paperwork on time. Sole traders do not need to perform these tasks.

For more information about director's responsibilities, visit: https://www.gov.uk/running-a-limited-company/directors-responsibilities and https://www.gov.uk/running-a-limited-company/company-annual-return.

Overall, limited companies have more paperwork and legal obligations to fulfil. It may be for these reasons that limited companies can be seen as more professional, as they are subject to more "checks and balances."

Partnerships and *Limited Liability Partnerships.* These businesses consist of two or more individuals sharing profits, management and legal responsibilities.

Social enterprises are set up to help people or communities and can register as sole traders, limited companies, partnerships, charities, co-operatives or CICs (Community Interest Companies) if the necessary criteria are met. Visit http://www.socialenterprise.org.uk/ for more information.

Registering your business with the correct organisations

Both sole trader and limited companies must contact *HMRC* (Her Majesty's Revenue and Customs) and register for *Self-Assessment;* HMRC's process for collecting taxes from the self-employed.

Self-Assessment tax returns can be completed online or on paper. You'll be given more time to complete yours if you choose the online option. There's a time limit for registration, based on when you started your business. The link below explains how to calculate your *registration deadline:* https://www.gov.uk/set-up-sole-trader/register.

Don't get on the wrong side of the tax man, check in order to avoid issues!

If you wish to form a limited company, you can approach Companies House directly via the Gov.uk website: https://www.gov.uk/register-a-company-online and register your company and its name for a fee of £12, or pay a *company formation agent* anything from around £15 - £150 to set the company up for you. Gov.uk lists a number of formation agents on its website - using one of these may be a better plan than trawling the web: http://bit.ly/1OtJe2p

If you are based outside of the UK, please contact your local state or government department for details of how to register your business.

Additional sources of information

HMRC offers information at:

https://www.gov.uk/government/news/webinars-emails-and-videos-if-youre-self-employed which includes dates of forthcoming webinars on record keeping and filing tax returns, links to advice based videos on YouTube, plus email services and several e-learning guides.

There's a Self-Assessment tax guide here: http://www.hmrc.gov.uk/courses/SYOB3/syob_3/html/syob_3_menu.html and a guide to business expenses here:http://www.hmrc.gov.uk/courses/SYOB3/syob_3_exps/html/syob_3_exps_menu.html

Business insurance

There are a range of insurance policies you can take out to protect your enterprise against legal action and claims for damages.
Costs will vary depending on factors such as your age, location and the nature of your business.
Levels of cover range from around £500,000 into the millions, depending on the size of your business, the level of risk you're exposed to, and the amount of cover you require. Let's look at a few examples:

Business contents insurance. Don't assume that your home insurance policy will cover business items, such as expensive computer or home office equipment. Check with your home insurer to make sure you're covered.

Public liability insurance covers you and your business for compensation claims and legal expenses in the event that a customer or member of the public makes a claim against you for property damage, personal loss or injury.

Employer's liability insurance protects your employees and covers you against damages if a claim is made against you by an employee. Employer's liability insurance is required by law if you hire staff, however, this may not be required if the worker:

- Is based in a different country, or is in the same country, but does not work in your office
- Uses their own equipment
- Has their own insurance
- Does not have a long-term contract
- Is not directly supervised by you

Professional indemnity insurance cover will help you defend claims relating to inadequate advice, negligence or errors and the cost of rectifying mistakes, including legal costs, compensation and expenses.

Selecting a reputable insurance company
https://www.comparethemarket.com, http://www.gocompare.com/, http://simplybusiness.co.uk/insurance and http://www.confused.com/ are some of the larger online price and quote comparison sites for business insurance.
Axa; https://us.axa.com/small-business/ (US)
and http://www.axa.co.uk/insurance/business (UK),
Hiscox; http://www.hiscox.com/small-business-insurance/ (US)
andhttps://www.hiscox.co.uk/business-insurance/ (UK) and Direct Line for business https://www.directlineforbusiness.co.uk/ are some of the big names in the general insurance market.

Policy inclusions and exclusions can vary significantly between companies.
Read the small print carefully and if necessary, request clarification before signing up!

Accounting, budgeting and keeping financial records

It's a good idea to keep a log that you can continually update as you learn more about the running costs associated with starting and maintaining your business. You can use this to create a rough budget for running it on a monthly basis. Log all one-off, monthly and annual costs, and any other business related expenses that arise.

Keeping financial records

Make sure you claim the cost of hiring staff and other allowable businesses expenses. Keep your receipts, invoices and bank statements as evidence of your business transactions and for your self-assessment tax returns and pass copies to your accountant, if you plan to use one.

In the UK, financial records must be kept for a period of six years. If you're based in another country, be sure to find out how long you must hold your financial records.

Bookkeeping, (financial record keeping), will help you keep track of all your receipts and expenses. This can be done using spreadsheets, mobile apps or accountancy software such as *Xero*, https://www.xero.com/uk/ or *Freshbooks*, https://www.freshbooks.com You can do your own bookkeeping, or hire a bookkeeper or accountant to help you.

You can confirm which expenses you are allowed to claim via your accountant, HMRC or the Gov.uk website. Here is a list of common business expenses that you can claim for if you go down the self-employment / sole-trader route; https://www.gov.uk/expenses-if-youre-self-employed/overview.

According to the Gov.uk website, the major categories of expenses you can claim for include:

- Office costs, e.g. stationery or phone bills. You may also be able to claim some expenses if you work from home.
- Travel costs, e.g. fuel, parking, train or bus fares.
- Staff costs, e.g. salaries or subcontractor costs.
- Financial costs, e.g. insurance, accountant's fees and bank charges.
- Costs of your business premises, e.g. heating, lighting and business rates.
- Advertising or marketing expenses, e.g. costs related to running your website and online advertising.

Expenses for limited companies work differently and you can find out more about the accounting process for limited companies and the expenses that can be claimed here:

Expense management apps

If you choose the do-it-yourself route for bookkeeping or accounting, there are some excellent free and paid apps available under "receipts", "expenses" or "accounting" searches via Google Play, The App Store and other app marketplaces. A few examples include *Toshl*; see http://apple.co/2adDKS9 for Apple device users and http://bit.ly/LGBgtG for Android users, https://toshl.com/ and *Finance PM* for Android, http://bit.ly/2aj9cxT via the Google Play store.

These are great time-saving devices because they make it so easy to log expenses as soon as they arise, so your bookkeeping is always up-to-date.

Fig 4, images i-iii. The Toshl mobile app

   i)   Adding expenses

The labels in the apps are quite versatile, so you can customise them to suit your own purposes.

ii)   Setting a budget

Budgets can be set within some apps, so the app subtracts your expenditure from the funds you have available.

iii) Exporting or printing your expense and accounting records.

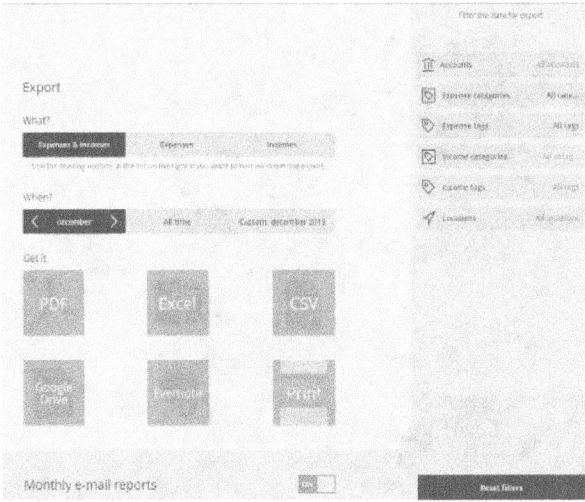

In most cases, expense apps will allow you to generate a spreadsheet based on all the expense entries logged in the app. You can see from the example that *Toshl* offers several ways to export your data, whilst *Abukai expenses,* http://bit.ly/2axnWpd will let you photograph an expense and will turn this into a line item in a spreadsheet, which can be emailed to you.

Finding an accountant

Many accountants offer free initial consultations to discuss their services and charges. You can find an accountant via the ICAEW - the Institute of Chartered accountants in England & Wales at:
http://www.businessadviceservice.com/.

A brief word about VAT

I won't go into a great level of detail about *VAT (Value Added Tax)* and *VAT registration* here, except to mention that sole traders and limited companies must become *VAT registered* once the business begins earning over £83,000 (correct as of March 2016). Being VAT registered involves collecting and paying VAT to HMRC on a quarterly basis.

There are some advantages to registering to pay VAT, even if you haven't hit the £83,000 threshold. These include creating the impression that you are a larger company, (possibly making it easier to do business with larger VAT registered organisations) and being able to claim VAT back on your own business expenses. In January 2015, a new type of VAT, *VAT Moss, (VAT mini one-stop-shop)*, was introduced. As a result, VAT due on the sales of digital services from businesses to consumers based in the EU must be charged at each customer's local rate of VAT. The £83,000 threshold applies to VAT Moss too. There is also a simpler, *flat rate VAT scheme* for businesses:

https://www.gov.uk/vat-flat-rate-scheme/overview.

VAT and VAT Moss overviews can be found here:

https://www.gov.uk/vat-returns/overview.

Next, let's explore your idea...

CHAPTER 2
How to develop your idea...and 5 market research exercises

"Learn from yesterday, live for today, hope for tomorrow. The important thing is not to stop questioning."
- Albert Einstein

In this chapter:

- Why do people pay for products and services?
- Guided market research exercises: competitor research, market positioning and more
- Let's crunch some numbers!
- Google search secrets
- Project pitfalls
- Creating simple business plans
- Free resources
- Chapter challenges

Why do people pay for products and services?

When people pay money to a business, they're paying for services or products that give them what they *want* or what they *need* by either: i) solving a painful problem that they'd like to get rid of, or ii) bringing them a benefit or result that they would like to receive.

The more wants and needs your product fulfils, the more powerful your *proposition* (the idea you're intending to bring to market) becomes. Usually, the bigger the problem you solve or benefit you help people to obtain, the more you can charge for delivering it.

Can I share another quote with you? It comes from an American businesswoman called Alice Foote MacDougall, who once said:

"In business you get what *you* want by giving other people what *they* want."

Which problems and "wants" can you solve, and solve well?

Make customers your obsession

Walking in the shoes of your customers is essential when creating products and services. For over ten years I've managed and been part of teams that have delivered software applications used by members of the general public and specific consumer target markets; including pregnant women, people trying to manage debt and people trying to buy their first home and for business users too, including journalists, accountants, administrators, sales teams, human resource departments, trainers and customer service functions!

I have spent countless hours observing and interviewing people in order to create better products, trying to find the answers to questions such as:

- What annoys them?
- What makes their lives easier?
- What are their needs, priorities and preferences?
- *Why* are those things so important to them?

*Study the people that you hope will become your customers, so you can understand how they think and behave - the goal is to transition from **your** way of thinking to **theirs**.*

Spend time with the people who are eventually going to use your product, because:

- *You can't create a product to satisfy a group of people if you don't understand what they want, what they value and why they value it.*
- *If your product isn't useful, usable or valuable enough, you won't be able to build a solid customer base of people who will use or pay for it – and without that, you will find it difficult to build a viable business.*

In the Introduction, we saw that the number 1 reported reason for startups failing in the *CB Insights* study was a lack of real need for the product and reason number 9 was ignoring the customer!

Neglecting your customers is one of the biggest pitfalls and ways to lose money on your venture. Seek to understand them, carry out market research and take into account their wants and needs. Regularly check-in with your target market as your product evolves to be sure that you are still on track to deliver a product that pleases them.

Have you ever been given a gift that wasn't right for you?
Maybe it was something that the person who gave it to you would love to receive. Trying to sell a group of people the wrong product is similar to this, but not only is the "gift" not right, but you're also expecting them to use *and* pay you for it!
To "nail" the perfect gift, you either need to know and understand the other person well, or ask them what they want directly!
We'll talk about how to interview potential customers, also known as*prospects* in chapter 3.

You are at the start of an ongoing scientific experiment...

In order to maximise interest and sales, you'll want to make sure that you have:

- Identified a *problem* to solve - ideally a large or very painful one!
- Identified a group that needs a solution to that problem (i.e. your *target market*.)
- Come up with a *solution* that is *attractive and acceptable* to your target market.
- Identified a *method* to deliver the solution to your target market (either yourself or via a 3rd party) in an effective, economical and profitable manner.

Try not to assume that you have the 100% "right" product or service idea straight away. Confirm that your theories and assumptions are correct and fine-tune them as you go along.

Investigate different ways of presenting and delivering your product or service to your target market and modify your plans until your idea is "ready" to be delivered the way your customers want it, which makes it easy and convenient for them to do business with you.

In other words, let your customers shape your vision.

One definition of entrepreneurship is "organising and managing an enterprise, usually with considerable initiative and risk."

You can reduce the uncertainty and risk linked to your venture by *gathering data, seeking evidence, asking questions* and *making decisions based on what you learn. Don't rely on assumptions or guesswork!*

In the next chapter, we'll talk about how to identify your target customer(s) and their wants and needs, and how to level-up your market research efforts by speaking to some of them. However, before we get to that, let's review some key questions.

There are five important questions to ask yourself

Whether you want to sell a product or service, or to open an online or physical store (or sell via someone else's), here are some questions to ask yourself about the market that you're considering:

1. **What is the size of your market?** Is it big enough to support a business?
2. **How sustainable is your idea?** What kind of longevity do you think your idea has?
3. **What is the health / stability of your market?** Is the market experiencing growth, or declining? Look for opportunities that will provide your business with a good foundation for growth.
4. **Who are your competitors?** How many are there? What do they charge? How well are they are serving the market? (Note that if there are a lot of competitors in the market, this can be a good sign as it means there's a lot of demand.)
5. **What about the bigger picture?** Your business will be impacted by events in the wider world. What impact could external factors have on your business venture and what could you possibly do about this?

Let's start gathering the answers to all these questions.

A guided market research exercise

An initial assessment of demand

Here are some simple, but powerful market research exercises you can do to assess the idea and market that you're considering.

Are you ready to get started? If this isn't a good time, please set yourself a bookmark and come back to this section later.

Time required: 30+ minutes, per exercise, depending on how long you spend on each one.

Materials required:

- A device connected to the Internet and a web browser for searching (e.g. Internet Explorer, Google Chrome, Safari, Firefox, etc.)
- A pen and paper, spreadsheet or other method for recording notes.

Objectives: To assess the levels of demand, opportunity and risk associated with your idea, before investing too much money and effort into it. By following the steps here, you will be able to gather information that could be used to refine your initial idea further.

Here's a worked example. <u>It can be applied to any idea</u>, but let's imagine that you wish to build some **computer game** software. You want to see what types of computer game are most popular before you decide on a course of action.
Follow along with me using this example, or complete the exercise based on your own ideas and area(s) of interest.

Google Trends and keyword tool exercises

Google Trends, https://www.google.co.uk/trends displays *trends* in the use of search terms over time (rather than providing figures). It's possible to search for global trends and local trends by changing the search filters available at the top of the page. You can compare up to 5 different *search terms* at once and can search within a specific time-frame.

At the top of the screen, you can see that I've set my regional search to United Kingdom. My search covers the last 12 months and I've chosen to look at Web Search trends as opposed to image, news or the other search options available. (See the blue bar at the top of the image, far right.)

Fig 5. A comparison search using Google Trends, based on web searches from July 2015 - July 2016

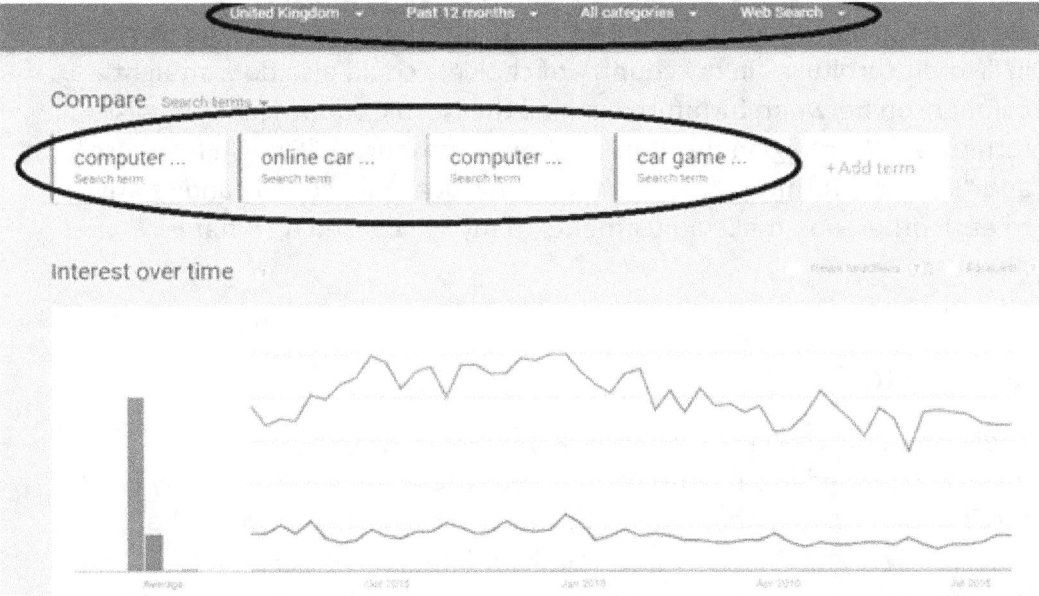

The boxes with the blue, red, yellow and green bands represent the four terms I've decided to compare and the bar and line graphs give an instant visual of their relative popularity.

In this example, I searched for computer games (with the blue band) as a benchmark and then decided to search for different types of computer game to see which search terms are most popular.

You can see that the term online car games (the red band) is the second most popular term, whilst the search terms represented by the yellow and green bands barely register on the graphs.

Persevere with your research until you are able to select a computer game or car game sub-genre that looks promising. There are many combinations of search terms you could try if you were looking for car games; "formula 1 racing games", "road race games", "car simulation games" etc.

*Look for ones with a **consistent or upward trend** in popularity over a period of time.*

The premise is the same whether you're planning to sell Nordic furniture, antique vases, web development services or luxury chocolate. Use Google Trends to break these high-level topics down as I did in our computer game example. So for instance, after searching for the trend in "Nordic furniture" in my country of choice, I could also do a straight comparison between furniture from all the Nordic countries - "Swedish furniture", "Norwegian furniture", "Danish furniture", "Finnish furniture" and "Icelandic furniture", assess the trends both individually and relative to each other, and make adjustments to my idea based on what I discover.

Keyword tools

There are tools you can use to check the relative popularity of *keywords* used in searches on the web. These tools are generally used for *SEM (Search Engine Marketing)*, which companies use when they wish to pay a search engine like Google or Bing to advertise their businesses by displaying them in people's search results. However, they can be used to gather a lot of useful information, even if you're not intending to pay for SEM. The services below all provide *keyword volume data,* so you can see the phrases that individuals and businesses are searching for online, and the numbers of people running those types of searches. Do further research (and new keyword searches) on any phrases that you find interesting and keep a note of the number of search results that you get. A few examples of these tools include:

Instakeywords; http://www.instakeywords.com/

The *Google Keyword Planner* tool, which is part of *Google AdWords;* used for *SEM* paid advertising to help companies rank highly on Google, https://adwords.google.co.uk/KeywordPlanner. (You may need Gmail and AdWords accounts to access this tool.)

Wordtracker; https://www.wordtracker.com/?splash=true

Wordstream.com; http://www.wordstream.com/keywords/

Fig 6. Running a keyword search for the term "computer games" using the Wordtracker tool

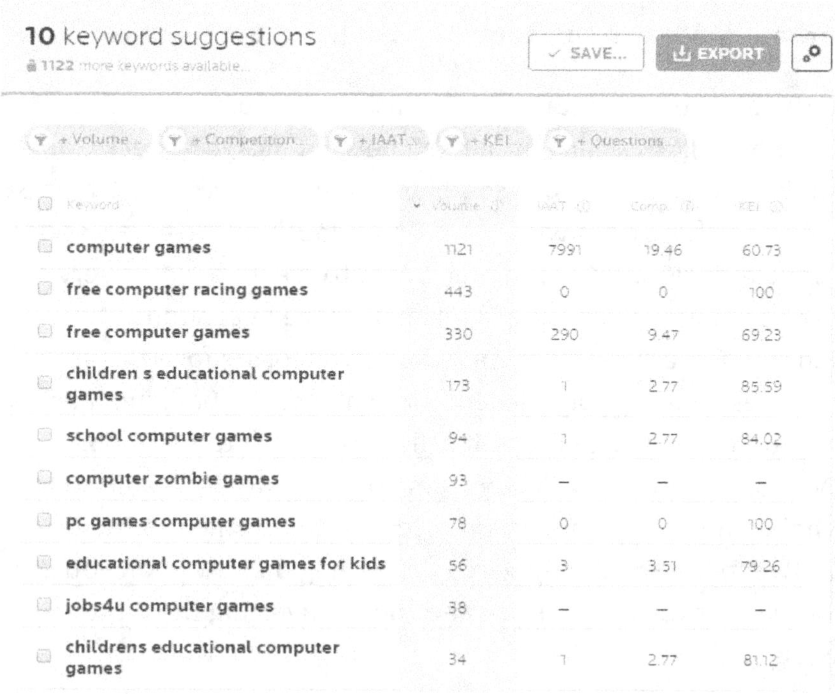

10 keyword suggestions

1122 more keywords available...

SAVE... EXPORT

+ Volume... + Competition... + IAAT... + KEI... + Questions...

Keyword	Volume	IAAT	Comp.	KEI
computer games	1121	7991	19.46	60.73
free computer racing games	443	0	0	100
free computer games	330	290	9.47	69.23
children s educational computer games	173	1	2.77	85.59
school computer games	94	1	2.77	84.02
computer zombie games	93	–	–	–
pc games computer games	78	0	0	100
educational computer games for kids	56	3	3.51	79.26
jobs4u computer games	38	–	–	–
childrens educational computer games	34	1	2.77	81.12

Before we move on, let's clarify the meaning of the column headings shown in the Wordtracker example above. This information will come in handy if you want to pay for SEM in the future.

Volume. The number of times a keyword has been searched for in the previous month.

IAAT (in anchor and title) shows how many web pages on the Internet have a given keyword in both the title tag (the title of each search result) and anchor text (the clickable text in a web link).

Competition. This number ranges between 1 and 100, and represents the number of optimised web pages on the Internet for each keyword.

(The higher the number, the more web pages there are that contain the keywords.)

A high *KEI* indicates keywords which a lot of people are using when they search, but which have a lower *competition* in terms of the number of web pages that contain these keywords, measured on a 1 to 100 scale.

This is your safe space to brainstorm ideas and test out theories...

There's no risk and you can indulge your business building fantasies! Ever dreamed of selling Italian leather satchels in Chicago? Check Google Trends and then do your keyword searches. Want to stock Nike trainers and need to know if the ones with the green swoosh or the blue swoosh are more popular? See what's trending. Want to create a dating service and wonder how many people are "looking for love in London"? Now you can find out! For a full-time business, you're looking for at least 10,000+ searches a month for a decent-sized market, depending on how much your product or service costs. It's also important to remember that not everyone searching will buy from you. You won't be able to tap into the whole market and *conversion rates* on web traffic can be anything between 0.5 and 3% upwards depending on how good you are at attracting visitors to your website and then converting them into paying customers.

So, what happens if the search volumes look good? Let's crunch some numbers and do a spot of *financial forecasting*!

Let's imagine that I'm planning to sell comics via my own website:

If I conservatively[1] estimate [based on my keyword research] the number of searches done by people looking to buy *Flash Gordon* comics at **5,000** searches a month in [insert the countries that the traffic is coming from[2]] and I can conservatively convert **1%** [3] of the total amount of traffic that visits my website into **paying customers** using [social media, SEM or other methods for driving traffic] and I charge an *average* of **$10** per comic, then I can make **$500 per month.**

5000 searches per month x 1% (0.01%) which is your slice of the pie from the number of searches per month in your desired locations) x $10 = $500 per month.

So the formula is: Monthly earnings = Number of available buyers (based on the number of monthly searches in your desired locations) **x** conversion rate (in %) **x** the amount you charge for the item.

[1]It's far better to underestimate than to overestimate!

Always aim to *overestimate your business costs* and *underestimate your business income*. If the figures don't cover all your expenses when you do this, then beware!

[2]I'd assume that these searches will come from countries where people speak the same language as you, since you're probably not going to have a copy of your website translated into Spanish, French, Arabic and Japanese, for example, if you're an English speaking American citizen!

Of course, you *could* have a huge English speaking fan base in another country (and you *could* get your website translated), but this example gives you a basic idea of the things you'll need to consider.

[3]The average *conversion rate* is approximately 2%.

Now you have this formula, you can scale your projections up or down and plug in different figures, either adjusting the conversion rate, the amount you charge, or the total number of available buyers by focusing on a larger market. It's worth noting that a larger or more diverse market *may* require more social media effort, SEM, marketing or advertising spend, a deeper knowledge of local markets - and more resources to handle customer care and *fulfillment* activities to get your products into your customers' hands. (You can always try expanding your territory little-by-little to test the water, if you have any concerns.)

To get a projection of your first 12 months' earnings, you could start to think about how much you expect to earn in your first 3 months, 6 months, 9 months and after your first year trading, taking into account your monthly running costs and one-off set-up costs. This will involve making some assumptions, for example that your conversion rate will increase as you learn what works best for your business. Just don't forget to think about **how** you will make these improvements, otherwise you'll have a goal, but no strategy in place to achieve it! As you work through this exercise think about the actions you will take that will make the difference:

Will you network like crazy and seek referrals and Joint Venture (JV) partnerships, become a whizz on social media, create a killer blog or other top-rate content to attract customers, pay for online or offline advertising (in local papers, or via Google, Bing, Facebook, Amazon or other means), sell on a busy online marketplace, SEO optimise the heck out of your own website, build a huge email list of interested parties and focus on email marketing, learn how to milk the media and PR "machine" or will you pick up the phone and hustle for sales?

Phew! That's quite a few options and the right answer will be a combination of the above. Start with a few activities that you're willing to commit to and believe are worth the effort, carefully monitor your success with them and go from there. Joining quality mastermind or support groups will be fantastic for speeding up your learning curve in terms of discovering what works and what doesn't.

Of course, you may also choose to have affiliates promote your product or service for you. At the end of the chapter, I've provided a list of resources that includes some affiliate links.

Competitor research and market positioning exercise

There are other quick ways to assess your competition or to refine your idea.

Let's look at ways to compare products, services and competitors and we'll run through a 5-step process using the mobile app market as an example.

This exercise can be applied to any idea (product or service) in any market, whether you want to write a book on a certain topic, open a restaurant or whatever it may be - so long as there are review sites or discussion forums that are relevant to your area(s) of interest. A number of links are provided below, so you can select your area(s) of interest.

The idea is to *model success* and to see how you might *reverse engineer* successful businesses or products to see what they are doing that is working well for them, rather than trying to "reinvent the wheel."

Examples include: *SiteJabber*, a site which collates reviews of online businesses; https://www.sitejabber.com, *Angie's list*, a US site for reviewing businesses; https://www.angieslist.com,*Reviewcentre*; http://www.reviewcentre.com, *Trustpilot*; https://trustpilot.com,(US) https://uk.trustpilot.com, (UK) *Revoo*; https://www.reevoo.com and *Feefo*; https://en.business.feefo.com are all popular review sites. Yelp.co.uk (UK) and Yelp.com (US) are also popular review sites. If you are planning to sell products, then *Ebay*, *Amazon* and *Alibaba* will also be worth looking at to research your chosen market. To compare mobile apps, browse the app marketplaces (see the worked example below) and if you want to sell software including SaaS / web applications, try the big software comparison review sites such as *Capterra*, http://www.capterra.com, *G2crowd* https://www.g2crowd.com and *TrustRadius*, https://www.trustradius.com for reviews on web / SaaS (Software as a Service) applications.

You may also find Google reviews available for some businesses.

In the section below we will work through some examples of how to assess what others are doing well - but also what you might offer that might be different, or better than the competition.

Researching a market

In this guided example, I'm going to investigate the market potential for a mobile app. However, as we've discussed, this could just as easily be an investigation into the products for sale on Ebay or Amazon, or a search on a review site. Use the same 5-step process in each case, starting from the big picture and drilling down to investigate gaps and opportunities in the market, the product or service itself, the competition currently providing the product or service, and thinking about where your business might fit in. Once this has been done, you can review what you've learned and decide what action(s) you will take.

1. **Review some app categories / consider the range of products (or services) that exist in your area(s) of interest.** If you're considering different product ideas, it can be helpful to see all the available options! Take a look at the *categories* of app available at Apple's App Store, https://itunes.apple.com/en/genre/ios/id36?mt=8 or Google Play Store, (click the "categories" button in the top menu area); https://play.google.com/store/apps?hl=en_GB, or alternatively, visit the app stores via your smartphone.

2. **Look for gaps or areas of dissatisfaction.** Run a keyword search and look at the apps, products or services most similar to the one(s) you have in mind. Select 3 or more competitors' products with *overall* ratings of between 3 and 4.5. These are apps in the range from "O.k." to "very good." For each one, drill or scroll down and look at the proportion of ratings from 5* to 1*. The 5* reviews should tell you what pleases customers most about the product, whilst 3* and 4* reviews reflect positivity, but indicate that some customers feel the product "could be better" or has just fallen short of the ideal for some reason. Look at what needs improvement and *note the reviews with specific information included:* what disappointed the customer, or stopped them from giving a better review? The 1* and 2* reviews obviously reflect dissatisfaction. What do reviewers really dislike, or consider to be significant issues with the product and why? Look out for trends.
From what you have observed, is there an opportunity to offer a superior product or to position a new app so it covers functionality or services that have been neglected or overlooked?

3. **Assess how good your competitors are at customer service.** Look for feedback relating to customer care. Do they respond positively and professionally to customers' feedback?

Do they even respond at all? What issues have you identified? Could you offer better customer care than them?

4. **Where do you fit into this picture?** Now that you have this information, you'll have more ideas about how to *position* your app. This may include things you should do (and avoid doing), the likes and dislikes of customers and what is important to them. These could be functional gaps; where the products or services do not deliver all the things that customers would like, or in the *way* that they would like, customer service issues as discussed in point 4, issues relating to the presentation, or general quality of the product or other elements that annoy people. You may even be able to see reviewers' photos - this will give you an idea of the demographic that use the app, their ages and whether they are male or female. Does there seem to be a *type* of person that uses these apps? In other words, are you able to identify a demographic? What do they say they use the app for? *This information is all absolute gold in terms of market intelligence and consumer research!* It's also a good idea to note the keywords that your competitors use in their product descriptions. Do you need to use the same ones? Are there others you could use that would bring your product up in the search results of your target customers? Your keywords are vital in marketplaces like Google Play, the App Store, Ebay, Amazon and other sites, so take care not to miss important keywords that would increase your visibility. Try out different keyword combinations and see which products come up in each search. When you start to see search results that you feel your product or service fits in with (and could compete with) you're on the right track. A **pro tip** here is to create a keyword for companies or products that you specifically want to "chase," if the rules of the marketplace allow this. This is actually very common - have you ever searched for Business A on Google, only to find Business B ranking highly in search results which include Business A's name? Cheeky? Maybe. Effective? Yes!

5. **Review, reflect and take the next step.** Keep a record of your observations and ideas so you can easily review and compare all the information you've gathered. Armed with this information, there is an opportunity to build an app (or other product or

service) which is appealing in all the right ways, but avoids the worst elements of your competitors' products. In addition to quality, also consider what new or exciting twists you could provide to make your app unique, so it stands out within its category.

Fig 7. Star ratings for a game available in the Google Play Store

Google research secrets

Get the most from Google with these less well-known search tools:

Get serious with the *Google advanced search,* https://www.google.com/advanced_search. Include exact words or phrases, or choose to exclude specific keywords from your search results. You can add a + (plus) sign next to words that must appear, and a − (minus) sign next to words that you *don't* want to see in your search results.

Turn Google into your virtual assistant with *Google Alerts,* https://www.google.co.uk/alerts, useful for monitoring the latest news on your topic of interest. Put it to work collecting data from across the web for you 24 hours a day, 7 days a week!

Enter the keywords you're interested in, enter an email address, click on the "show options" menu and specify how often you want to receive notifications and you're set. Once your product or service is "live" you could set up an alert to see who's talking about it!

Fig 8. Put Google Alerts to work for you and receive alerts via email or RSS

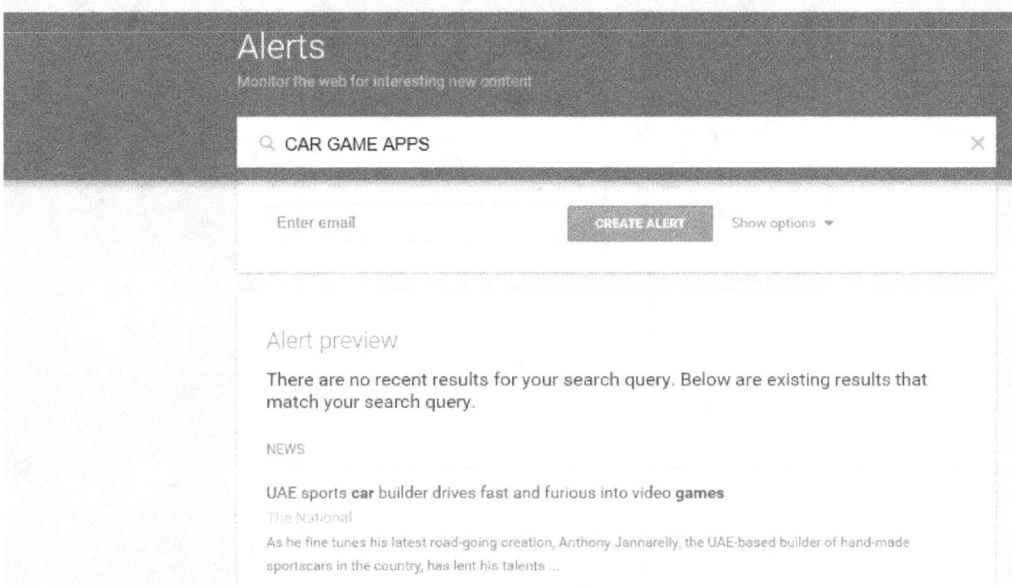

Did you know you can insert currency symbols, @ signs, hashtags and asterisks * into your Google searches?

Asterisks fill in the blanks for you, so for instance a search for the *"most popular * in New York"* will bring back results that tell you about all sorts of things that are popular in that city, replace New York with a relevant city, country or even a continent based on your requirements.

Use hashtag and @ searches to locate useful information *on social media sites* and see if you can find out what companies are charging by running a search that includes a $ £ €, or other currency symbols!

Here's a link to a nice summary page that explains all the options that are available!

https://support.google.com/websearch/answer/2466433?hl=en

Google Scholar,

https://scholar.google.co.uk/schhp?hl=en&as_sdt=2000b will help you locate research published on your topic of interest including journals and research from leading institutions. Set up an *alert* so you can receive email notifications about your preferred topic(s).

Fig 9. Find the latest academic research on your topic of choice using Google Scholar

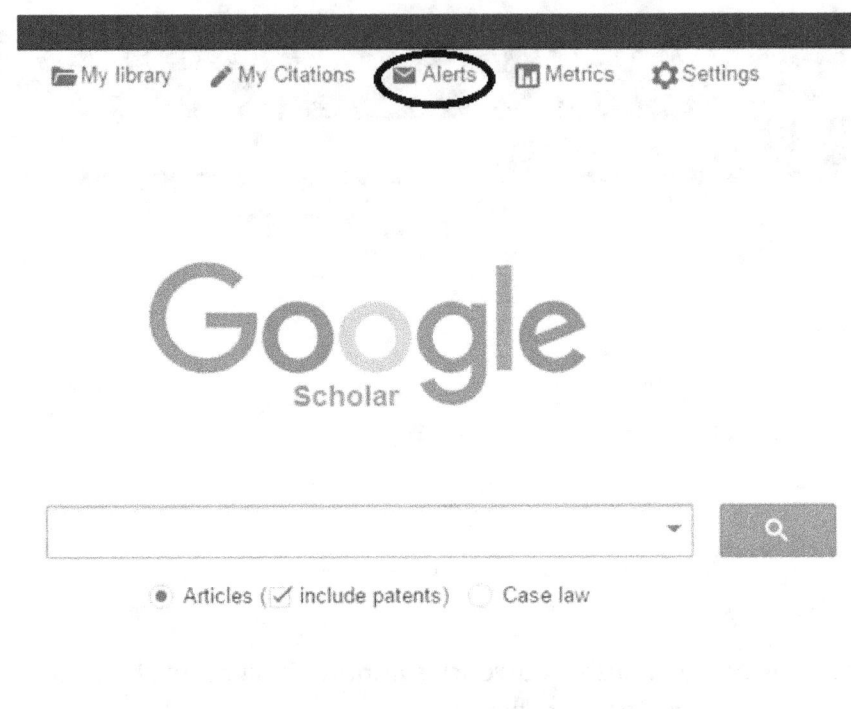

Google's *Consumer Barometer* can be used to review high-level trends across populations. It also provides insights into different consumer groups and their behaviour and usage trends across smartphones, desktops and tablets: https://www.consumerbarometer.com/en/

Other sources of market and business intelligence data
Libraries can be a fantastic source of market data that may not be free online. Some have access to the databases of big players in the business intelligence and market data industries. Contact your local library to see whether you can access it for free. If not, some of the companies offer an initial free trial:

Bureau Van Dijk provides company information and financial data for the UK, Europe and Australia via their *Fame* and *MINT* products, http://www.bvdinfo.com/en-gb/our-products/company-information/national-products.

To find global data, including the USA and Asia Pacific, consider using the *Orbis, Amadeus, Osiris* or *Mint Global* databases: http://www.bvdinfo.com/en-gb/our-products/company-information/international-products and http://www.bvdinfo.com/en-gb/our-products/company-information/international-products.

COBRA provides thousands of business guides, factsheets and reports, http://cobra.cobwebinfo.com/.

IBISWorld provides market research data, business and industry reports, http://www.ibisworld.co.uk/.

Key Note is a leading business intelligence company, https://www.keynote.co.uk/.

MarketLine Advantage profiles major companies, industries and regions, http://marketline.com/.

Analysis tools for businesses: PESTLE and SWOT exercises

PESTLE analysis
External factors beyond your control can have a big impact on your business. Products should evolve as customer demands and preferences change, but also as the business environment changes.
Larger companies will make sure they have staff, (often people like me) to do research and analysis to make sure they are aware of and prepared for impending challenges, but there is no reason why small businesses can't take precautions too!

The *PESTLE* acronym covers 6 types of external factor that you should consider and stands for - *Political, Economic, Social, Technological, Legal and Environmental.*
You may wonder how these factors might affect you, but at any time your customers' ability to buy from you might be affected as a result of changes in the landscape in any of these 6 areas.

PESTLE is a useful reminder about outside influences that could help, or hinder your venture and it is better to "get in front" of these wherever possible.

Social trends, fashions and fads can affect the popularity of different goods and services and businesses that were budget friendly did especially well during the global *economic* crisis.

Changes of government can mean changes to the laws which affect business operations. When running a business, you will need to pay attention to the *legal* requirements related to the payment of tax, as well as compliance with rules and regulations related to businesses in general, and within your sector, or area of commercial focus.

Make sure that you are aware of any legal requirements or regulations that you will need to comply with as a business. In some sectors these can be quite onerous and it may save you time and money if you are aware of them in the early stages of building your business!

For US citizens, the US Small Business Administration (SBA) provides useful links on regulations here: https://www.sba.gov/starting-business/learn-about-business-laws.

Those in the UK may need to contact a trade association, or similar bodies for advice. However, this free business support helpline may be able to direct you to the right place to find all the regulations that apply to you: https://www.gov.uk/business-support-helpline.

There is also a Gov.uk business regulations page here: https://www.gov.uk/government/policies/business-regulation. (Use the *Organisation* filter on the left-hand side of the page to help you pinpoint the right information.)

Technological advances can have a big impact on businesses, so watch out for new trends. These may result in websites or software needing to be modified or updated in order to keep pace with (or to take advantage of) changes that might benefit your business. Technological changes can affect businesses significantly - every time Google, Amazon or Facebook change their algorithms or policies, companies of all sizes scramble to adapt and restore the status quo.

Environmental issues can have an impact on businesses too. There are delivery companies offering "green " delivery slots to customers which are more environmentally (and fuel) friendly, and environmentally-aware consumers may pay attention to the materials that businesses use to package their products.

Next, let's look at some simple ways to use *PESTLE* when doing online research.

Using Google to carry out PESTLE research

You can't necessarily control external events, but keeping an eye on events and changes in the wider world *might* give you enough advance warning to take the necessary precautions. To avoid nasty surprises, run some Google searches in the following areas and select the variation(s) that you are most interested in:

- "Compliance" or "legislation" or "law" or "regulations" + [your area of interest]
- "Technological advances" or "technological trends" or "latest technologies" or "new technologies" + [your area of interest]
- "Economy" + [your area of interest]
- "Growth industry" or "growth market" or "growth sector" + [your area of interest] and "industry decline" or "market decline" or "sector decline" [your area of interest]
- "Demographics" or "statistics" or "trends" or "data" + [the current or previous year] + [your area of interest].

You can see where I'm going with this. These keyword combinations will retrieve useful information, but you can experiment with other phrases too.

Keeping up-to-date

To stay abreast of the latest developments in your sector, try subscribing to the e-newsletters of a few respected magazines, groups or blogs relevant to your area(s) of interest to make sure you're among the first to receive important industry news. Some accountancy firms are great at keeping their clients up-to-date, so sign up with a few who offer this service - even if they don't do your accounts! You can always find a few from your nearest town or city and drop them an email to enquire about their services and fees and from there you can ask to be added to their mailing lists. You could also set up *Google alerts* to send you email reminders about *PESTLE* related topics.

SWOT analysis

Another quick but effective tool you can use for assessments or decision making is the *SWOT analysis.* Grab a sheet of paper and write down the *Strengths, Weaknesses, Opportunities and Threats*(SWOT) associated with the topic you wish to review and then assess the positive and negative factors associated with it.

SWOT analyses can be used to review:

- A product or service
- Your own skills and abilities, or those of your team
- Your idea(s)
- Different competitors
- Different customer groups or markets

They can also be used to make comparisons. When you do your SWOT analysis, remember to include any new information you have gathered during the course of this chapter.

An example
Strengths might include receiving consistent positive feedback about your product, or product idea and its features, or having specialist or in-depth knowledge that gives you a competitive edge.

A lack of experience in your industry of choice might be classed as a *weakness*.

An *opportunity* could be that you've discovered a gap in the market that you believe your product could fill.

A Threat might be a limited budget to establish your product or service, or discovering that an existing player has also identified the gap and will be developing or upgrading a product to meet the demand.

If you get your keywords right, *Google Alerts* can be great for notifying you about opportunities and threats. You could even monitor competitors, or competing products by name!

Fig 10. SWOT analysis table. https://commons.wikimedia.org/wiki/File:SWOT_en.svg, Xhienne

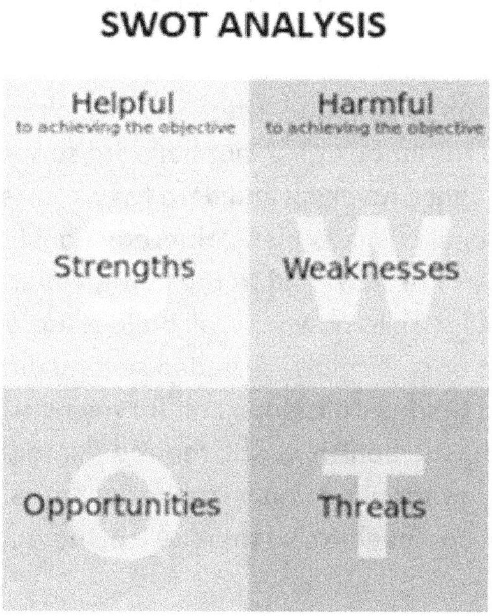

SWOT ANALYSIS

Helpful to achieving the objective	Harmful to achieving the objective
Strengths	Weaknesses
Opportunities	Threats

Comparing SWOT analyses for different ideas can provide insights you might not otherwise have had.

Dig into this further - some weaknesses or threats may make an idea a non-starter, so you'll need to think about:

- Your ability to deliver a quality product
- The resources you have to get your product out to the market quickly (financial, or otherwise.)
- Whether your opportunities outweigh your threats
- Whether weaknesses can be overcome
- Whether there are enough strengths to make your venture worthwhile
- How your strengths can be maximised

Creating a business plan

We've covered a lot of ground in this chapter, so this seems like the right time to capture all the thoughts, insights, observations and financial projections in a *business plan*.

Please seriously consider creating one if you haven't done so already. If you're planning to go to the bank for a loan, expect to be asked to produce one.

Business plans are probably right up there with watching paint dry in terms of things we'd rather be doing, but here are some plans that you are likely to find thought provoking and dare I say it, interesting! In contrast with traditional business plans, the *Lean Canvas* and *Lean business model canvas* are short and to the point, yet contain enough detail to help you understand how you will build a successful business around your product or service. I've included several different versions here. I've worked on them with clients, and for my own ventures and I think they're brilliant. The bank may still require a traditional plan, but you can transfer the information you've gathered into a more formal business plan later if you need to, so there will be no duplication of effort.

- Business model canvas; https://strategyzer.com/canvas/business-model-canvas?url=canvas/bmc
- Lean canvas; http://3daystartup.org/wp-content/uploads/2014/04/lean-canvas.jpg
- Business model canvas; http://www.witszen.com/wp-content/uploads/2013/05/Business-Model-Canvas.png

You now have a range of tools and methods for gathering data that you can use to assess your ideas, both now and in the future!
In the next chapter, we'll be identifying the right customers for your business and I'll explain how you can go beyond the figures that the keyword and business intelligence tools provide and gather insights directly from "real" people.

Don't miss the Develop Your Idea! Planning board. I've created a visual representation of all the topics that we've discussed in a tool called *Trello* that you are free to copy if you sign up for a free Trello account:

http://www.mylanderpages.com/donthireasoftwaredeveloperuntilyour eadthisbook/free-resource-2-trello-boards

RESOURCES

Creating your own website - website builder tools and landing pages

You may be thinking about setting up a website, or even several landing pages to give yourself an online presence. There are a number of website builder tools that do not require any code to be written, and you can use them to build yourself a website from scratch. Those below are all well-established players in the market and are quite user-friendly:

Wix, http://www.wix.com/
Weebly, http://www.weebly.com/
1and1, https://www.1and1.co.uk/
Squarespace, https://www.squarespace.com
WordPress, www.wordpress.com/
Moonfruit, http://www.moonfruit.com/
Zohosites, https://www.zoho.com/sites/website-builder.html

They all offer a large selection of website templates and the majority have plug-ins available which will add extra functionality to your site. Plug-in examples include online review plug-ins, the ability to add PayPal buttons to the site to transform it into an e-commerce store and price plan comparison widgets (see the links and examples in chapter 8), which are used to display the service and pricing options available to customers. Double check that the template you select is *responsive* and will re-size for mobile.

Give your chosen site(s) my 30-minute test.

If you can't make progress quickly and without getting very frustrated within that period, it's time to switch, or if you can afford to, you could outsource the work!

Landing page apps

Landing pages are 1-page websites used to perform a specific purpose such as promoting or selling a product or service, or to collect sales leads.

Launchrock, http://launchrock.com/ and *Kickoff labs* https://kickofflabs.com/ focus on providing services for startups.

Other landing page tools include:

Instapage, https://instapage.com

Landingi, https://landingi.com/

Leadpages, https://www.leadpages.net

ActiveTrail, https://www.activetrail.com/

Landerapp, https://landerapp.com/

All the tools offer a free trial, and prices start from around $29 per month, apart from ActiveTrail which currently starts from a budget-friendly price of $7 per month and supports email and SMS marketing. Most of these apps will let you create *as many landing pages as you like* under the same account, and as a rule, most will allow you to connect domains you have already purchased to a limited number of landing pages.
Some also offer A/B testing functionality, which lets you compare two different versions of a landing page by displaying them both to customers on rotation. A page showing the effectiveness of each one will be available for you to review within the app.

My tip would be to sign up for 2 or 3 tools on a trial basis with the functionality you want. (Most will give you between 14 and 30 days for free.) See how much you can achieve with each one in a set period of time, then decide which product is right for you.

Online marketplaces

In addition to having your own web site or landing pages, there are many places for you to sell your products online:

Etsy, for handmade, vintage and unique items,

https://www.etsy.com/uk/, https://www.etsy.com

Gumroad helps creative people to sell their products online,

https://gumroad.com/

Shopify, can support you whether you sell online, via social media or want to embed a shopping cart into your website,

https://www.shopify.co.uk,

https://www.shopify.com/

Clothing, music, art and more can be sold via Storenvy,

https://www.storenvy.com

Set up an online store with Jumpseller, https://jumpseller.com/

Popular Wordpress plug ins for ecommerce include, https://woocommerce.com *and Easy Digital Downloads*

https://easydigitaldownloads.com/

Create your own store and sell digital downloads with E-Junkie,

https://www.e-junkie.com

Buy products in bulk and resell them individually to consumers, or sell in bulk to other businesses via Alibaba, https://www.alibaba.com

Don't forget *Amazon, Ebay, Google Play* and the *App Store*!

If you're interested in making sales via affiliates, or earning money as an affiliate, then the Amazon affiliate network, https://affiliate-program.amazon.com/, *Clickbank,* http://www.clickbank.com/affiliate-network/ *and e-junkie ,* http://www.e-junkie.com/ej/affiliates.htm *may all be worth considering.*

Get them done and check them off! Chapter 2 challenges:

- ☐ If you weren't ready or able to complete the market research exercises covered in this chapter, set yourself a reminder to come back to them.
- ☐ Create at least 1 "lean" business plan. Give them a try! They'll really get you thinking, and help you see where the gaps in your approach are.
- ☐ Reflect on what you've learned in this chapter. What conclusions can you draw and what action(s) will you take as a result?
- ☐ Commit to trying to think like a scientist and consistently seek data and evidence to confirm that all is really as it seems. Does your idea need to be adapted in any way(s) in order to make it more useful, or relevant? How?
- ☐ Note the action(s) you'd like to take, based on the market research that you've done during the course of this chapter and set due dates for them.

Everything you've learned will be wasted knowledge if you don't follow up!

Download the entire set of chapter challenges for this book in the form of a work book, with an activity log to help you keep track of important tasks: http://www.mylanderpages.com/donthireasoftwaredeveloperuntilyoureadthisbook/Free-resource-1

CHAPTER 3

Creating customer profiles, and your first customer interviews

"The more you engage with customers, the clearer things become and the easier it is to determine what you should be doing."
- John Russell, former VP, Harley-Davidson Europe

In this chapter:

- Identifying your target customers
- Customer profile creation exercise
- Finding customers to help you validate your idea
- Top 10 do's and don'ts for running customer interviews
- Sample customer interview questions
- Free resources
- Chapter challenges

In the previous chapter, we talked about approaching the development of your product like a scientific experiment. You can advance forwards, or stop to make corrections based on what you've learned, and use data and evidence to help shape your ideas. Now, we're going to look at how to gather data that will identify the right customers for your product and help you understand what their priorities are.

Creating customer profiles

When developing a product, creating profiles that represent your target customers is a beneficial exercise, whether you're planning to serve consumers or other businesses.

You may have come across avatars before - they are usually cartoon-style representations of people. *Customer avatars* (a.k.a. *customer profiles* or *customer personas*) may be paired with a written profile to help you visualise your *target customer.* This is a person that you have identified as being *most likely* to buy from you. Your target customer has *exactly* the type of problem(s) that you can solve and their wants and needs fit well with your product. **Your *target market* is a broader group of potential customers.** Imagine looking at a huge crowd (your target market) from a distance through a telescope, and then zooming in on one individual (your target customer.) It's much easier to try and understand one person's needs than it is to focus on a multitude of people at once. Another common term for people who might buy from you is *prospects*.

Here are some examples from *YouGov*, an international market research firm. Note how they combine the image of the avatar with written details to create the overall customer profile. They have a fantastic profiling tool, https://yougov.co.uk/profileslite#/ which looks at audience profiles across different companies. Here are some YouGov profiles for readers of *The Independent newspaper* and for *Instagram* customers:

Fig 11. YouGov customer profile for customers of *The Independent* newspaper.

The Independent

Customers of The Independent

GENERAL INTERESTS
- POLITICS
- INTERNATIONAL NEWS
- EXHIBITIONS

NICHE INTERESTS
- WOMEN'S ISSUES
- CULTURE & THE ARTS
- EDITORIALS & COMMENT
- HUMAN RIGHTS CHARITIES
- WRITING

FAVOURITE DISHES

HOBBIES & ACTIVITIES
- WRITING
- TREKKING AND HIKING
- GOING TO MUSEUMS AND GALLERIES

FAVOURITE SPORTS
- CYCLING
- CRICKET

MOST LIKELY PET
- CAT

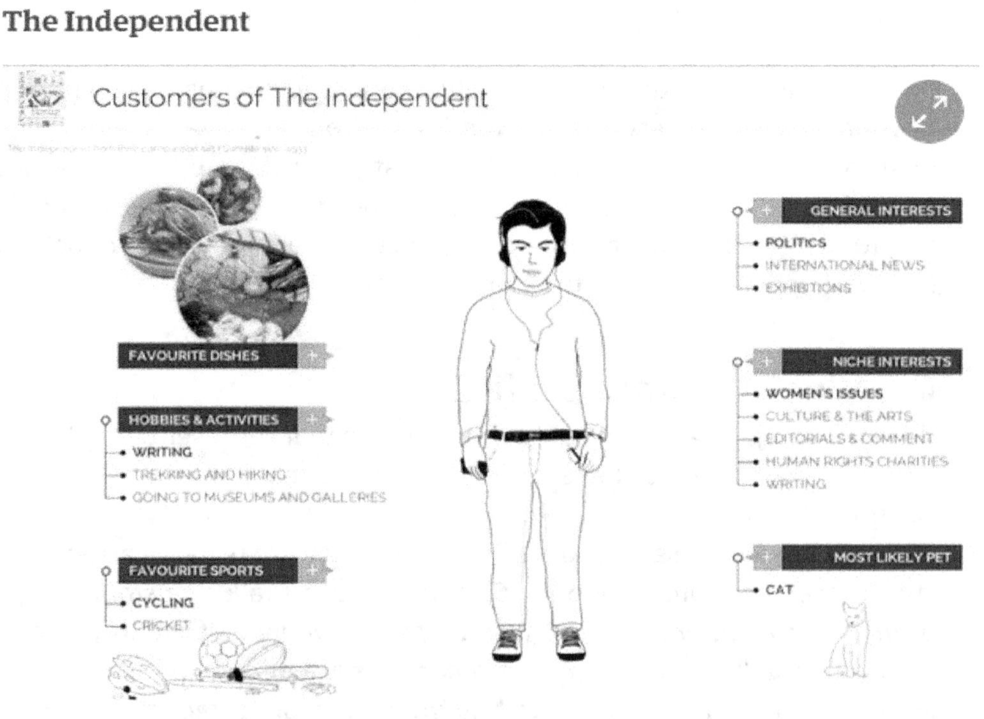

YouGov Independent Customer Profile Photograph: YouGov

Fig 12. YouGov customer profile for Instagram customers.

Companies pay agencies thousands of pounds to create customer avatars for them, because they create a focal point which helps them hone their products. You have an opportunity to get these benefits free of charge!

A strong customer profile will help you focus on the types of people that you need to serve and communicate with to build your business. The insights you gain will make it worth the effort.

Consumer classification tools

You may find it helpful to approach this activity from several angles. There are companies that analyse and segment consumer populations and help businesses understand how to "speak" to their audiences in the right ways via marketing and advertising. They achieve this by providing *consumer classification* data.
US and general classifications:
http://www.strategicbusinessinsights.com/vals/ustypes.shtml
UK focused classifications: http://acorn.caci.co.uk/downloads/Acorn-User-guide.pdf

Consider the classifications that both these links identify and use them as inspiration as you create your own customer profile(s). As you look through them, you may be drawn to certain descriptions or may recognise that your target customer comes from a group that has already been "classified." If this is the case, there may be a wealth of information about that group online that you can use to augment your knowledge. Look for research, statistics and trends, news articles, blogs and academic papers as a starting point. Use the Google search tricks from chapter 2 to do some advanced searching and to set yourself alerts.

Customer profile creation exercise

Now it's your turn! There are a few things to note before you start:

- You can create profiles for multiple avatars. If this feels like the right thing to do, create them, take a careful look at them all, decide which ones feel like the *best fit* for your product and focus on those.
- If anyone you've spoken to so far has been enthusiastic about your product idea (especially if they say they would consider buying it), capture as much information as possible about their hobbies, habits, and lifestyle and consider using them as one of your avatars, at least until you have reason to believe that there are other profiles that would be more suitable.
- Use the YouGov profiler tool to search for products or brands close to your vision of your own product and see what you can learn! Remember that everyone lives within a context. **What customers are doing when they** *aren't* **using your product also matters.** *Learning about their preferences and the products and services that they like to use could have a bearing on* **how you present and position your own product.**

Now start to imagine the type of customer that you wish to attract. Really try and see them in your mind's eye. Let's get into the spirit of this!

Fig 13. Customer profile form.

Review the forms below and complete the relevant parts:

Full name of avatar	Create a realistic name for your avatar which you feel suits their personality.
Gender	Could your avatar be of any gender or are you targeting a specific gender group? Does any particular gender feel like a better fit for your product?
Age	How old are they? State a precise age. Your target market will have an *age range*; your target customer should have an *age*.
Family / Relationship status	Are they single, married or cohabiting? Do they have children? If so, how many and how old are they? Depending on what your product is, even the gender of their children could be important.
Education	Did they finish school? Attend college or university? Do they have a degree or more advanced level of education such as a master's degree or Doctorate?
Occupation	What do they do for a living? Are they "blue collar" workers, elite professionals or somewhere in between?
Job title	This will be useful if you're planning to create a B2B (business to business) product rather than one for consumers (B2C) and want to target specific people such as HR Managers, CEO's or Marketing Directors.
Annual income	How much do they earn and how much disposable income do they have available to spend on products and services like yours? Are they looking for budget products, mid-range or luxury ones?

Home life	Where in the world does your avatar live? Do they live in an urban area, in a commuter town or out in the countryside? What kind of neighbourhood do they live in? Do they rent or own their own home?
Hobbies, groups, community activities and memberships	What do they do in their free time? Do they have any hobbies, or belong to any online, or offline groups, clubs or societies? (Once you know this, you'll have a much better idea of where to find your target customers, where to advertise or market your product and where to go when you need to gather feedback on your idea or product.)
Favourite newspapers and magazines	Which newspapers and magazines do they read? Is this done on or offline? (If you're considering paying for ads in newspapers, this information could be very useful. News publications know their reader demographics, so ask for their reader statistics before you pay for advertising space.)
Favourite websites	Where can they be found online? Which social media platforms do they use? (This will give you an idea of where to find your target group, where to advertise or market your product and where to find people to help with market research and product testing.)
You might also wish to consider the following:	
Vehicle	Does your target customer own a car? Ride a scooter or a bicycle? What make and model? How many vehicles do they own?
Industry sector	This may be relevant if your customers will be other businesses.
Company size	If you are looking to sell to businesses, what size of business are you targeting?

The inner world of your target customer

Let's spend a little time thinking about your target customer's inner world. This is another exercise to help you get "in tune" with your customer's problems, and how they think and feel.

Fig 14. The inner world of your target customer.

What are your avatar's problems, frustrations and challenges?	
What are their fears and concerns? **What, if anything troubles them?**	
What benefits are they hoping to receive?	
What are their hopes, goals and aspirations?	
How well does your product fit into this picture? *Does your product idea need to be adapted to better suit the target market?* *Or is there a target market that would better suit your product?* **If you've had any a-ha moments, that's excellent! Please write them down.**	

You can download a copy of this form and the customer profile form, with space to add your own avatars' details at:

http://www.mylanderpages.com/donthireasoftwaredeveloperuntilyoure adthisbook/5-customer-profile-avatar

Creating an avatar to represent your target customer

Here are some examples of avatars that can be used to represent consumers or business customers:

Fig 15. Freepik avatar creator tools. Male avatar creator.

http://www.freepik.com/free-vector/male-avatar-creator_822151.htm

Fig 16. Freepik avatar creator tools. Female avatar creator.

http://www.freepik.com/free-vector/woman-avatar-creator_824042.htm

Fig 17. Freepik avatar creator tools. Business team avatar examples.

http://www.freepik.com/free-vector/business-team-avatar-collection_874660.htm

You can choose a cartoon-style avatar as seen in the Freepik designs, but you can also use an image that you feel represents your target customer, or even do a hand drawing.

Practical applications
You should now have version 1 of an avatar and customer profile to work with!

Understanding what they want, value and hope for will help you to create a product well-suited to their needs and an effective and targeted marketing plan in the future.

Now, you can start making decisions that take your avatar(s) into account, including shaping the way your product evolves. This might feel a bit odd at first, but thinking like this will allow you to make some very clear decisions about what is and isn't right for your target customer(s).

Ask yourself:
- "How would my avatar, [insert avatar name] feel about this? What would they expect?"
- "How would my avatar like to perform this task?"

- "How could my product make life easier and more convenient for my avatar?"
- "What part(s) of my product will my avatar value the most?"
- "How could I make using my product a more enjoyable experience for my avatar?"
- Would my avatar like this social media post?

Continue to update your customer profile(s) as you learn more about your target customer(s). They should evolve over time. This is just the beginning!

Remember that you're testing theories...

Remember to consider everything you *think* you know about your customers to be a theory or assumption until you have enough evidence to be sure. The earlier you find out that things may not be as they first appeared, the easier it will be to adjust your plans and make your product into what it needs to be. Stop and reflect, then work out what to do next. You may need to make some adjustments, or abandon certain plans altogether. This could be disappointing, but it isn't a failure - you could have lost time and money in pursuing the wrong type of customer or building the wrong type of product. Agile and Lean principles support the concept of "failing fast", then making adjustments based on what has been learned, and trying again.
This is what entrepreneurs do!

Finding target customers to interview

Evaluating an idea or product through the use of customer interviews or product testing sessions can cost as much as several thousand pounds *per session,* if set up by professional *recruitment or market research agencies.*

These agencies will find people from your target market that are willing to be interviewed. Some agencies will run the tests for you, others will expect you to run them yourself.

This may or may not include venue hire costs (if you would like a venue to be provided for the testing sessions) plus an incentive payment ranging from between £30-100 for each person that is interviewed as payment for their time.

If you don't have the budget to hire a specialist company, then you'll need to find your own participants and run your own interviews.

Now you've gone through the avatar creation process you'll have a list of possible places where your target customers might be found, including membership groups and profiles on social media sites. At the time of writing, these were the most popular social media sites in the US and UK:

- Facebook
- YouTube
- Twitter
- LinkedIn
- Instagram
- Pinterest
- Google+
- Snapchat
- Tumblr
- Reddit
- Flickr
- Meetup.com

If you know of any specialist membership sites, forums or groups that might be relevant, try those too. If not, try Googling for "top membership sites, forums or groups" then include extra keywords which describe your area(s) of interest.

Ease into the task of finding people to interview by starting with friends and family and asking for introductions to *their* friends and family. Consider attending networking groups and events where you can speak to people who may be in your target market face-to-face.
Meetup.com https://www.meetup.com/ and
Eventbrite, https://www.eventbrite.com/ may be able to help you find local events in your area, regardless of where you're based.

When reaching out to people you know, or have been connected with:
Create social media posts, let people know what you need and ask them to share your messages.

When people respond, try and get at least some face-to-face interviews arranged if you can - it will be easier to build rapport in person and you will be able to observe people's facial expressions and body language as you talk to them about your product idea. You could offer to treat people to a beverage or lunch when you ask for their time.

When reaching out to people you don't know:
Try joining relevant groups on each social media platform that you use. Post within the group, and if possible drop people in the groups short messages which are relevant to them, using their name if possible, so your communication doesn't feel impersonal and generic. Explain who you are and what assistance you're looking for. If there is anything you can exchange in return for their time and effort, let them know that too. Some people will be willing to help; others will want to know how getting involved will benefit *them.* Not everyone will have the time or even the interest in helping, but from a statistical perspective, the more people you ask, the more will say yes!

This article contains some useful tips for reaching out to people online: https://www.linkedin.com/pulse/20130624114114-69244073-6-ways-to-get-me-to-email-you-back.

Ask people how they'd prefer to be contacted and try to be as flexible as possible. Be prepared to make contact via phone, Skype, Google Hangouts or using other methods.

What should you ask your target customers?
Gather as much data as possible, so you can refine your product idea or *proposition* (your proposed solution to the problem) through:

- Understanding more about their needs and problems.
- Learning whether the target customers you identified *really are* your ideal customers - are your avatar(s) accurate or not?
- Discussing *how* you might solve the problem (if you already have an idea of how the product might work.)
- Looking for trends - specific likes and dislikes, and any commonalities. What do people strongly agree or disagree about?

- Testing the waters to see if people would pay for the product. If so, how much and if no, why not? Under what circumstances *would* they pay for it?

It's not just what you ask, but how you ask it...

Training as a coach and working as a market researcher forced me to work on getting rid of some of these commonplace habits. Do your best to avoid them when you're interviewing, and you'll get much better-quality responses.

Here are my top 10 do's and don'ts when running customer interviews and testing prototypes:

- **DO be organised.** Have a notepad to hand or ask for permission to record the conversation. Listening to recordings will also help you improve your interview technique. Prepare a set of questions to ask in the form of a script. Ideally you should be consistent, asking *every customer the same set of questions* so you can compare them more easily later. However, changing the *order* of questions can be really beneficial to the interview process. Do a few interviews, see what works, then update and reorder your script if needed. Run through any exercises and questions you've prepared a few times to check for issues before your first interview and read your script out loud too - interestingly, you'll pick up on different issues via your auditory sense than you will just by reading it.
- **DO put people at ease before you start.** Explain there are no right or wrong answers and that you would appreciate their honest opinions and feedback. (When testing a prototype or product, assure them that you are testing *it*, and not them!) Ask some warm-up questions; a summary of who they are and their occupation can be a good way to start. Ask them how they are or how their day was, then recap on why you're speaking to them. Don't tell them *exactly* why until the end, otherwise you risk introducing *interview bias*. This happens when an interviewee says what they *think* you want to hear to please you, or to avoid offending you. That would count as a *false positive*.

- **DO be prepared to repeat yourself.** Let people know that they should ask you to repeat any questions that they feel are unclear.
- **DO ask open questions...and ask for full explanations.** There's nowhere left to go if someone responds with a "no," so ask *open questions* and start your sentences with *Who, What, When, Which, Where, How* and *Why* and not "Do you?", as this can close conversations down quite quickly. Other good questions include, "How often do you...?", "When was the last time you...?", "What made you say that?", "How does that work?", "Can you tell me about...?"
- **DO be encouraging.** Keep saying things, like "Uh-huh", "Keep going", "Tell me more." This is especially important if you're on the phone, to confirm that you're listening and are still there! If people don't explain the reason for their comments, ask "What makes you say that?" or "How come?" to prompt them to go into more detail.
- **DON'T lead people.** *This is very important.* Saying things like "Would you like a ... [your product]?" and "Would you pay $20 for a product or service that does... [whatever your product or service does]?" are pushing someone in the direction you want them to go in. You could end up with false positives if you lead people to the answers you want. You want to know what they would *really* do and what they *honestly* think.
- **DON'T fill the silence**. Ask a question...*and then say nothing!* Don't try and fill in the silence by asking another question, or ten! If you know anyone who has a habit of asking many questions on top of each other, I'm sure you'll agree that it can be a bit maddening after a while, *so give each person space and time to think.* If you ask multiple questions at once you'll break their concentration, which disrupts the process. Silence sometimes makes people feel nervous, but over time you'll feel less self-conscious about it. *Nothing fatal happens during a silence and actually some really great insights can come during those moments.*
- **DON'T fire questions at people - or interrupt them.** Don't direct questions at people like machine gun fire, or make them feel like they're on trial and facing a prosecuting lawyer! Create a calm

atmosphere, listen carefully and don't interrupt! If another question pops into your mind, write it down so it doesn't distract you and get back to listening, otherwise you might miss something important.

- **DO push for negative feedback.** Always ask what people *don't* like. You'll want to find out as many negatives about your proposition as possible, *before* you invest in creating your product or service and to allow you to make essential adjustments.
- **DO make it a positive experience.** As the product develops you will need regular feedback to stay on track. Try to make the interview experience as pleasant, professional and interesting as possible so people are happy to talk to you again in future when you have more to discuss or show to them.

Running customer interviews

To begin, create a set of interview questions to help you gather *information* and *evidence*. Shall we start with a few examples?

A customer interview about computer games

The benefits of games and the problems they solve include alleviating boredom, escapism, relaxation (or stimulation) and social contact and a sense of belonging in the case of team games. These are my *hypotheses* on why people play games. Now I'll need to prove them *and* decide how the things I learn should shape my product development decisions.

When starting the interview:

Take down the person's details - name, age (or age bracket), job title and details of hobbies and websites visited regularly to help you build up a picture of each customer. Compare these with your avatar and customer profile. What do you learn?

Begin with some general questions about the problem that your product solves as a "warm up." It would probably be inappropriate to ask people directly whether they play games for escapism or social contact, but you could ask how people spend their free time and when they play games and expand the conversation from there.

Ask about people's daily schedules - do they drive or take public transport to and from work? How do they spend their time during the commute? When they get home, what happens? If they try to relax and wind down, how do they do this? What hobbies and activities do they pursue after work and at weekends? Find out about where gaming fits into their life currently.

In this example, you're looking to identify all the free time and windows of opportunity for playing games and how long each window lasts, because you want to know *how much time people have to play* your game and to understand their *current gaming habits*. There's no point creating an immersive game that needs an hour to complete if your target customers have just 15 minutes of free time here and there throughout the week and don't have much time to play at weekends.

Next, ask them to tell you about *the last time* they played a computer game. Asking about the last time that a person performed an activity (whether it was shopping on Ebay or Amazon, ordering food online, hiring a freelancer etc - whatever your product or service of choice might be), is a question used by professional researchers. It's a great question because the answers you receive should be grounded in reality and based on fact. You'll have a better chance of learning about what people really *have done,* rather than what they *might do.*

Topic of discussion	Sample questions
Regular habits / frequency of use	How *many* games did they play in a row? Which day of the week did they play? Find out if this is the norm, or not. What time of day was it? Find out if this is the norm, or not. How *often* do they play during the week? What about at weekends? How *long* do they play for?
Preferred way of using the product / service	Which device did they use to play the game? Do they play on any other devices? Which, if any, is their preferred device and why?

Specific questions about the product or service being discussed	What type of game was it? What happened? What was the end result? Was it a positive, neutral, or negative experience? Why was this the case? Which services, options and settings available within the game did they use? (Ask them to tell you all the ones they use on a regular basis.) This may lead to you gathering other information on the topic.
Preferences, motivations and competitor research	What do they like about gaming in general? What are the pros and cons of the games that they play? What are their *favourite* types of games? Why do they like those games? What do they like the least about them? What do they find most annoying or frustrating? What is most important to them about these games?
Further exploration	If people can show you their games and walk you through how they play them, and their strategies, even better - this exercise is also about understanding the mindset, motivations and inner world of the person you're speaking to.
Gathering feedback about your own idea	If you're ready to do so, talk about your idea directly or indirectly and note the reactions of the person you are interviewing. Ask them to tell you what they like and dislike about the idea and why.

These questions can be adjusted to suit most topics, substitute your area of interest, whether it is a product or service.

Of course, products can be very different, so here's a second example:

A customer interview about a mobile app for scanning documents
Here's another example. If you wanted to create a document scanning mobile app, which allows the customer to take pictures of documents

with their phone and then share, upload or email them, you might start out by asking people what kinds of documents they receive and where they come from. From here, discuss each type of document they mention in turn, gathering as much information as you can.

You might also ask how they manage physical paperwork at home, how many letters they get each week, what types of letters they get, what they do with them and where they keep them. You'd explore what annoys or frustrates them about managing post and documents and investigate if there is anything time consuming about doing this.

Then you might ask about *the last* set of paper documents they received, what happened and how they dealt with them, what was complicated about the situation, how they solved the problem and what would have made the situation easier for them. Take down the names of any products they mention, so you can investigate any competitors. Ask for an opinion about these products and note down their strengths and weaknesses.

If you are ready to do so, talk about your idea directly or indirectly and note the reactions of the person you are interviewing. Ask them to tell you what they like and dislike about the idea and why. Note down all the ideas and suggestions that come up.

Note the words people use when they converse with you and stay alert for any slang or jargon used. As well as helping you to learn more about your customers, this information will be useful for marketing later.

Use terminology that your target market is familiar with to grab their attention.

Log and analyse your feedback

There's a simple analysis technique you can use to review all the feedback received, called Plus, Minus, Interesting, which I've adapted into an easy to use record sheet. You can download a copy of the Plus, Minus, Interesting (PMI) log:

http://www.mylanderpages.com/donthireasoftwaredeveloperuntilyour eadthisbook/Free-resource-3-pmi-log

Fill in each column as follows:

Plus. Note down all positive feedback and expressions of interest. Strong positive feedback would include comments like: "I really like it!" "That would be really useful, because…", "How much would you charge for this?" and "When can I get it?"

Minus. Write down all negative feedback or signs of disinterest in the product idea. If people say the idea would *not* be useful or solve their problem and if they dislike *the way* you propose to solve the problem, note this down.

Interesting! Note down any surprising feedback or information. This could relate to how people would like to use the product, insights gained or new ideas and suggestions that you receive. What do people value or get most excited about? How do they want to receive, or experience your product or service? How do they want to use the product? Also, note down the other products mentioned and any other information you gain from them, whether good and bad.

General notes. If you wish to create a product for businesses, note the industry sector, number of employees, turnover and age of the company. Note down what people say word for word and even the phrases they use. This is all excellent information to help you understand your customers. Keep a record of who seemed most interested in the idea and their age, gender and other things you know about them, so you can start to build up a profile of what type of person (or business) likes your product the most.

Get them done and check them off! Chapter 3 challenges:

- ☐ Download a copy of the customer profile and customer inner world forms and complete them. Create your customer avatar(s) and customer profile(s).
- ☐ Prepare yourself mentally for all types of feedback. How will you manage less positive feedback or suggestions, yet remain motivated, and open-minded enough to take away useful information?
- ☐ Create a plan for yourself and start doing customer interviews, so you can gather feedback about the product and test out the theories about your target market and avatar(s). Create a list of people you will interview, starting with people you know and

decide if you will reach out to others via social media or other channels that you have identified.

- ☐ Evaluate the feedback you've gathered. What have you learned?
  - What "a-ha" moments have come from reviewing all the data in your PMI log? (Get a copy of the log via the download link provided earlier in the chapter.)
  - What customer problems have you identified?
  - How will you use this information?
  - Do you need to adjust your idea to make it fit in more with customers' needs?
- ☐ Store all this information for future reference. Perhaps you could create a business research folder to hold your data...
- ☐ Update your avatar(s) as you learn more about how your market thinks and feels.
- ☐ Write down the actions you need to take based on feedback from your customer interviews. **Don't forget to update your business plan with any new information gathered whilst completing this chapter!**

Download the entire set of chapter challenges for this book in the form of a work book, with an activity log to help you keep track of important tasks:

Next, we're going to talk about *preselling* your idea!

CHAPTER 4
PRESALES AND RAISING FUNDS FOR YOUR BUSINESS

"While most startups who set up pages on Kickstarter, Indiegogo or a host of other crowdfunding sites are looking to hit a specific goal and then get started making their project a reality, a new crop of businesses are using the platform as a wholly different business model: selling their product before it exists."
- Harvard Business Review

In this chapter:

- The benefits of preselling products and services
- Crowdfunding options
- Alternatives to traditional bank loans

Now you've identified your target customers and have them at the heart of everything you do, let's look at how you might further increase your confidence that your product idea is attractive to your target market and that you're "on to something" good! As we've discussed, you'll want to reduce the risk of wasting time and money in creating a product that the market does not really want or need.

How do you find out whether your product idea is a "no", a "maybe", or a resounding "yes!"?

There are many smart businesses and business people that do not advocate spending a penny on product development until they are confident that:

1. The market is large enough to support a business. (See chapter 2.)

2. They understand a market's pains and frustrations. (Identify a problem and understand it well.)

3. They've identified ways to solve those pains and frustrations and possess (or are able to hire people with) the capability, skills and resources to deliver that solution. (Identify solutions and choose the most appropriate one based on market knowledge and available resources - whether these resources are yours, or come from other people or organisations.)

4. They understand what the product needs to be and do in order to make customers happy. (Identify the critical elements of your product that the market really values and offer these to your target customers as your first priority.)

5. They've identified customers within the market that like their product idea and are genuinely interested in it. (Gather hard evidence that indicates that your solution is a good match for the problem.)

6. **They've taken money in advance from their future customers in the form of presales.** (Confirm that people are actually prepared to part with their cash to get access to what you have to offer.)

Doing this research and validation work is a smart move because now the chances of success are greatly weighted in their favour! Which of these 6 stages would you most like to be at and which one would make you feel most confident when it comes to pursuing your goals? These stages may need to be revisited and fine-tuned, but isn't it useful to know what you could be aiming for?

We've already covered stages 1-5 in this book. All that remains is for us to talk about stage 6.

What exactly are presales?

Presales can help you assess genuine interest in your product or service. These are sales of services or goods before their release date in order to minimise the investment risk in creating the product - as we've discussed it's risky to create a product (especially an expensive one) until we know more about how well it might be received. Presales can also be used to fund the creation of the product in full or to contribute towards development costs. Do you think that the odds of success would be in your favour if you were able to achieve this?

Here are examples of several companies and industries that you know, who use the presales method all the time.

- **The house building industry / off-plan house sales.** When a customer buys into the glossy brochure provided for a new property development, when all that might exist is a hole in the ground, or where building work has started, but may not be finished for months or even years - that is a presale.
- **Consumer electronics / mobile devices**. Did you order your iPhone *before* it came out? If you paid in advance, you were a presale! Big presentations are often given, and Apple fans are whipped into a frenzy and pre-order because they want to be among the first to get the latest new gadget.
- **Consumer electronics / Games, gaming consoles and accessories.** What about the latest version of the Sony PlayStation? Did you pay up-front in advance for yourself, or a loved one? What about the latest games, or gaming accessories - waiting lists often exist for in-demand products, with people prepared to pay in full, or to leave a deposit in order to keep their place in the queue.
There are also a number of online shopping sites which allow traders to put their products up for pre-order and crowdfunding sites use this model too.

There is nothing "scammy" or dishonest about presales as long as you: i) Give people what you agreed to give them for the money they have paid and ii) If you return any monies paid in full if you aren't able to deliver on your promise.

If you'd like to investigate pre-selling in more detail, here are some points to consider:

- **Begin close to home.** Which family, friends and acquaintances need your product or service? Would any of them sign up to be your first customers?

- **Take a look at the major crowdfunding sites.** If you'd like to raise funds to build your product, Crowdfunding might be the way to go if you're happy raising funds from a large number of people happy to make a contribution to your venture. The top crowdfunding sites may change over time, but take a look at Kickstarter; https://www.kickstarter.com/, Indiegogo;https://www.indiegogo.com/, RocketHub; https://www.rockethub.com/ and GoFundMe; https://uk.gofundme.com/.
- **Read the small print.** If you want to go down the crowdfunding route, make sure you're familiar with each site's terms and conditions, fee structure and rules before you make a final decision about which one is right for you.
- **Model success.** Take a look at the campaigns on the crowdfunding sites and see how people with offerings similar to yours have pitched and positioned themselves. Look at the campaigns that are going strong and are on target to reach their funding goal and those that have raised funds in excess of their goal - and also those that are struggling to hit their funding target (or who have already failed to reach their target). Try to get an idea of what to do (and what to avoid). Some of the crowdfunding sites provide great videos and blog posts with tips on how to make your campaign a success. Here's some advice from Kickstarter: https://www.kickstarter.com/help/handbook/your_story and this YouTube video, from Indiegogo also has some brilliant tips. It's just over 3 minutes long and the tips and data insights at point 1:30 in the video are pure gold: http://bit.ly/29afJqb. *YouTube*, the online training website *Udemy* and *Slideshare.com* also feature advice on how to "win" at crowdfunding.
- **Take what you've learned and prepare an effective sales pitch.** Tell your story and your reason for creating the product and clearly outline what people will get and how the product will benefit them. Don't forget about your target customers and what you've learned about them, their interests and priorities. Use this knowledge to help you with your pitch. Include elements of this in your campaign to send out a clear and compelling message which will attract your target customers.

- **Get help to spread the word.** Email or message friends and family and get people you know (and the people they know) to support you across as many social networks as possible. The crowdfunding sites report that those who are consistent and have a good network of supporters helping them to spread the word are often the most successful. If you have a large network of contacts, this could really work to your advantage.

Your pitch will be a critical part of your crowdfunding campaign, so let's expand on the point above about preparing your pitch. Here are some straightforward sales techniques that you might consider using.

Try focusing on the *WIIFM, "What's in it for me?"* for your target customer group. Emphasise, (or even demonstrate) how you will either i) rid customers of their problems or ii) improve their lives and allow them to enjoy the benefits that you identified in chapter 3. This is a sales technique called *telling* a feature and *selling* a benefit, which keeps the focus on customers' needs. For example, factor 50 sun cream blocks the majority of UVA and UVB rays from the sun, but these are just the *features*. People appreciate the features of a product or service, but what they really care about is what it is going to do for them. Using sun cream correctly will greatly reduce your risk of premature aging and getting skin cancer. These are the *benefits,* and they're very powerful ones! It is these end results that the customer is paying for.

There is also a sales technique called *SPIN selling,* which is very popular. This stands for: Situation, Problem, Implication and Need-payoff. SPIN can be used to deconstruct the issues that your customers are facing and present an appropriate solution to them - your product or service! It would be fairly straightforward to prepare a written or verbal pitch using SPIN to make a compelling case.

You can find an overview here; http://www.sellingandpersuasiontechniques.com/SPIN-selling.html it's a basic page with a few sales prompts on it, but you can ignore those if you just want to read the content.

Other finance options

As an alternative to traditional bank loans, there are a number of organisations that may be able to help you obtain finance for your business. Take a look at these option(s):

Government funded loans:

Start Up Loans: https://www.startuploans.co.uk/

Angel Investors and venture capitalists (UK and US):

Angel Investment Network:
https://www.angelinvestmentnetwork.co.uk/entrepreneurs-home

UK Business Angels:
http://www.ukbusinessangelsassociation.org.uk/services-for-entrepreneurs/

Venture Central: http://www.venturecentral.co.uk/finding-investment/4583889654

CB Insights provide a list of the top 100 US venture capitalists. Click on the links under the column marked *Firm* to find out more about each VC company: https://www.cbinsights.com/blog/top-venture-capital-partners/

Peer to peer (P2P) lenders are another alternative to going to a bank for a loan. The larger players in the market include:

Funding circle UK: https://www.fundingcircle.com/uk\

Funding circle US: https://www.fundingcircle.com\

Zopa: https://www.zopa.com\

Ratesetter: https://www.ratesetter.com/

Equity crowdfunding allows startups and growing businesses to find investors and raise funds. In return, investors receive shares in the company.

Seedrs (offers "the crowd" equity in seed stage companies progressing towards building a prototype, or their MVP.) https://www.seedrs.com/raise

Crowdcube. Raise finance using their equity crowdfunding platform: https://www.crowdcube.com

AngelList (US) connects startups, investors, and those looking to join startups as employees: https://angel.co, *AngelList (UK)* https://angel.co/uk

Fundable offers equity and rewards based fundraising so you can offer investors rewards in exchange for cash, https://www.fundable.com/

EquityNet has been around since 2005 and will help you raise business capital, https://www.equitynet.com/

For an overview of the options available, *The Business Finance Guide* offers a comprehensive table of lending options for businesses at all stages of growth, with further information and videos available for you to explore each option: http://thebusinessfinanceguide.co.uk/finance-options/. Regardless of your location, this is an excellent guide to every type of business finance available, including some less well-known options. As always, check the small print before making any commitments!

Thank you for reading this book. I hope it has given you plenty of fresh insights, tools and ways to assess the pros and cons of progressing with a new venture. Please turn the page to find out what comes next!

THANK YOU

Thank you for taking the time to download this book. What comes next?

1. **Use the free resources** that come with this book. The download links are on the next page. The Chapter Challenges work book and Develop Your Idea! Planning board will really help you organise your thoughts and plan your next steps.
2. **Get your free bonus chapter.** This is a thank you gift for downloading this book. The link is on the next page.
3. **Kindly leave me a review at the page or site where you purchased the book.** I'd *really* appreciate it. Thanks in advance!
4. **Spread the word.** If you have friends, family or co-workers who would find this book useful, you can share the links below or post to social media. Sharing is caring! Here's the Amazon link for the ***Develop Your Idea!*** book:
   Enter the code B01N6GTOGM intothe Amazon search to find it, or use this universal link which whill show you the book in your local Amazon store:
   http://mybook.to/Develop-Your-Idea-exercises-validating-ebook.
5. **Progress on to reading: *Dont Hire a Software Developer Until You Read this Book***, for a step-by-step guide to hiring a developer and getting a software application built, if you have an interest in doing so!
   Enter the code B01LY5C1IK intothe Amazon search to find it, or use this universal link which whill show you the book in your local Amazon store: http://myBook.to/Dont-Hire-Software-Developer-Until-ebook.

With my very best wishes,

Kay

ABOUT THE AUTHOR

K.N. Kukoyi has a passion for translating concepts into professional software used by businesses and consumers worldwide, and has spent over a decade leading and working in technical teams, delivering mobile apps, websites and a range of other digital products for companies of all sizes, helping them to achieve their strategic goals through the use of software.

The author has also worked in market research, running consumer and business focus groups for clients and holds diplomas in Internet Marketing and coaching.

Kay has Diplomas in Internet Marketing and Coaching and enjoys coaching individuals and entrepreneurs to help them improve their performance.
She is the founder of Purposeful Products, a consultancy that provides business coaching services, and helps clients to transform their ideas into professional software products.

http://www.purposefulgroup.com/contact-us.html

hello@purposefulgroup.com

CREDITS

	Table of credits and references
	Introduction
1	Fig 1. CB Insights - The top 20 reasons why startups fail. www.cbinsights.com/blog/startup-failure-reasons-top/
	Chapter 1
2	Fig 2. Types of IP. Source, The Intellectual Property Office (IPO)
3	Fig 3. Patents and computer programs. Source, The Intellectual Property Office (IPO).http://www.ipo.gov.uk/blogs/iptutor/stem-patents-and-trade-secrets-part-1/
4	Fig 4. The Toshl app I-III, Appendix 1
	Chapter 2
5	Fig 5. A comparison search using Google Trends, based on web searches from July 2015 - July 2016
6	Fig 6. Running a keyword search for the term "computer games" using the Wordtracker tool.
7	Fig 7. Star ratings for a game available in the Google Play Store
8	Fig 8. Put Google Alerts to work for you and receive alerts via email or RSS
9	Fig 9. Find the latest academic research on your topic of choice using Google Scholar
10	Fig 10. SWOT analysis table. https://commons.wikimedia.org/wiki/File:SWOT_en.svg, Xhienne
	Entrepreneur definition, SMALL BUSINESS ENCYCLOPEDIA
	Chapter 3
11	Fig 11. YouGov customer profile for customers of The Independent newspaper
12	Fig 12. YouGov customer profile for Instagram customers
13	Fig 13. Customer profile form.
14	Fig 14. The inner world of your target customer.
15	Fig 15. Freepik avatar creator tools. http://www.freepik.com/free-vector/male-avatar-creator_822151.htm
16	Fig 16. Freepik avatar creator tools. Woman avatar creator.http://www.freepik.com/free-vector/woman-avatar-creator_824042.htm
17	Fig 17. Freepik avatar creator tools - business team avatar examples.http://www.freepik.com/free-vector/business-team-avatar-collection_874660.htm